Little House on the High Plains

on the

Sharilyn & Robbie Grayson *with*
Major General Carl G. Schneider
USAF (Ret.)

Traitmarker

A Traitmarker Books

Little House on the High Plains

on the

Growing Up Happy and Healthy
During the Dust Bowl and
World War II

Sharilyn & Robbie Grayson *with*
Major General Carl G. Schneider
USAF (Ret.)

Traitmarker Books
2984 Del Rio Pike
Franklin, TN 37069

ORDERING BOOKS FOR QUANTITY SALES
Special discounts are available on quantity purchases by corporations, associations, and others. For details, contact the author at the address above.

ATTRIBUTIONS
Interior Text Font: Minion Pro
Interior Title Fonts: Minion Pro
Editors: Sharilyn Grayson
Typesetter: Robbie Grayson
Cover Design: Drew MacArthur

BOOK PUBLISHING INFORMATION
Traitmarker Books
ISBN 978-1-68419-409-4
Published by TRAITMARKER BOOKS
traitmarkerbooks.com
traitmarker@gmail.com

Printed in the United States of America

CONTENTS

DEDICATION

...

These memories we preserve and pass to the next generation,
along with the family love we saw in our father, Carl Watson Schneider,
and our mother, Laura Kerlin Schneider.

Chapter One (1)

A Spacious Place

T ALL grass waves in gusty winds as far as the eye can see.

Deserts stretch in patchworks of rock and brush and sand over vast swaths of land.

Canyons house clear rivers, some broad and slow and warm, some deep and narrow and swift.

And no human eye sees any of them.

Long ago, before cities appeared, before farmers tamed some of the land, before ranchers claimed thousands and even millions of acres for their own, Texas belonged to itself. Antelope and buffalo grazed on it. Snakes and lizards baked in its searing sun. Tribes of native people wandered across it.

But no one owned it, and no hand shaped it. Rain-washed and wind-carved and sunbaked, it stretched from sky to sky in an ease of being that lingers in its wild places.

Then the Spanish came, Coronado and the other conquistadors who were hell-bent on finding fabulous cities of gold and gems. Bitter and disappointed at finding only fertile earth, they contented themselves with enslaving some of the native people and leaving missions to manage the rest. Across the West they marched, settling in the coastal plains and valleys of California and the deserts of Arizona and New Mexico and the broad plains and vast wilderness of Texas: places that reminded them of the Spain they had left.

There was war later, and then the Europeans came. And then Texas became a Republic. People transformed from Englishmen and Scotsmen and Germans straight into Texans, without becoming Americans first. They were leery of the Old World with its old ways, and they wanted a fresh start in a new place.

But Texas itself in a way was like the land of Old World fairy tales. There were cities, and there were small houses. But in between them, the land stretched in its timeless strength and beauty and wildness over unimaginable distances.

Though men owned those vistas, few men walked them.

Texas during the time of the Republic was a land of cowboys and ranches. The vast, grassy plains seemed meant to be the homes of cattle. For relatively little investment, men could make fortunes from the grass and the animals that ate it.

When Texas became part of the United States in 1845, there was little unclaimed land for the federal government to take and distribute to new settlers or use for federal parks and projects. Texas was in the hands of big ranchers and land barons. So while the rest of the West was being settled and farmed and shaped into cities here and there, Texas stayed wild and bare, the land of cows and the few men who tended them.

That changed after the Civil War and in the decades to follow. Slowly the owners of large ranches saw that as much money as they had made in cattle, more lay in the land itself. So they began to parcel out the land in sections of 640 acres or 320 acres or 160 acres. The land of even a small farm was so vast that it put a man miles from his nearest neighbor.

The home on the range was a lonely and desolate place for a man. But the new wave of farmers buying up former cattle ranches and converting them into farms were not the single, itinerant, fluid society of the cowboys and ranch hands. They were families, largely Southern American and European emigrants who brought churches and schools and government and society with them.

These institutions operated sporadically, when farmers and ranchers needed them or could spare the time to use them. Out on the plains, a farmer might go weeks without seeing a person who was not immediate kin to him. A visitor was a cause for celebration, a reason to use the best china, open the best preserves, and stay up late to hear the news.

And the milestones of life, despite their solemnity, became festivals. A wedding or a funeral united a community in joy or grief. A revival led by a visiting preacher brought families flocking together – not just out of concern for the welfare of their eternal spirits, but also for the soul comfort of being with one another.[1]

Part of the land newly opened to these sparse farmers was the Llano Estacado – a name that means "the staked plain" in Spanish.[2] People formulated different theories about why the Spanish chose that name for the place. Maybe the stakes referred to spiky wild yucca, or to the stakes legends said Coronado drove into the ocean of grass so that he wouldn't lose his way.

But if you look at the Caprock Escarpment rising three to five hundred feet above the desert wilderness below in sheer sides like the timbers of a fort, you see how the Spanish conquerors might have looked upon it and seen a palisade God had erected to safeguard the treasure of the plains.

When this wave of new farmers arrived, they lived for a time side by side with the rootless cowboys known for their independence and lawlessness.

Ernest Ragle, Carl Watson Schneider's nephew, heard a story from some early settlers of Lamb County (northwest of Crosby County) about the cowboys.[3] Hired to help a northern buyer select and separate the steers he wanted, they balked when he pulled out a whip and began to crack it to point out the steers. They knew better; they knew he was just asking for a stampede.

However, the cattle owners wouldn't stop him. They had to do business with him. So the cowboys just quit. They stayed at the site to hold the herd, but they weren't going to go anywhere close to that fool of a buyer.

For five days, they watched the owner ride a broken-down wagon horse to cut the desired steers out of the herd – none of them would loan him a good horse.

But with the dying of the million-acre ranches, the cowboys moved on – ever west, like many pioneers.[4] The first settler in what came to be known as Crosby County was Hank Smith, who arrived at Blanco Canyon in 1877. Following him in 1879, Quakers settled the community of Estacado, planning to make it a center of Quaker faith and even build a college.

Over the 1880s and early 1890s, though, farmers from East Texas and elsewhere swelled in numbers, overwhelming the Quaker colony.[5] A man named Ab Benedict bought a section of land on the rim of the Caprock Escarpment and created the town of Emma, giving away the deeds to town lots to anyone who would build a business on them. Benedict convinced Stringfellow and Hume to move a store there, and the townspeople built a school building also used for church when they could scare up a preacher. Tiny Hume named the town Emma after the woman he loved.

But Emma didn't last long. The arrival of the railroad thirty miles west in 1909 created the towns of Lorenzo, Ralls, and Crosbyton, and the townsfolk of Emma moved to them, abandoning their little city to the wilds.

The people who came afterwards, those who settled in Farmer and Ralls and Crosbyton, remembered and honored the first people who had tamed the land they inherited. One local poet, Flora Smith Dean, preserved the names and memories of the early settlers that she knew.

EARLY SETTLERS[6]

There's Uncle Em, and Lishe and John
And Uncle Bud they've journeyed on;
Old Aunt Mary, and Uncle Fan,
Dear Aunt Tek, and Grandma Van;
Uncle John Sawyer and Grandma, too,
Have gone to a land forever new;
Don't forget Joe, and Aunt Lucy, so dear,
Uncle John Noble, we miss you here;
And Aunt Ophelia, and Mother Cone,
Grandmother Ragle, all these are gone,
We miss your dear remembered faces
From their old familiar places;
Uncle John Kerlin, your beautiful life,
Will live forever, thru time and strife;
They left old ties, and settled here,
And made their homes, each pioneer;
Raised their children, in honor and truth,

Won the love of the aged and the youth;
They left their work upon the land,
Their old landmarks shall always stand;
Dear Old-Timers, 'tho you are gone
To a beautiful land, your deeds live on;
We remember you, always, in deepest love,
When we are Old-Timers, we'll meet you, above!

Among these pioneers who settled the land of Crosby County soon after Hank Smith were the Schneider family – and the Thorntons and Waites and Kerlins. Here is where the history of a state and a county meet the history of our family. Here is where we grew, and where we belonged.

Chapter Two (2)
Frederick Ernst &
Elizabeth Virginia Bare Schneider

GÖRLITZ, Germany lies on the Polish border in a region known as Silesia, and its roots are as much Polish and Czech as German.[7] It's a temperate, green land, flat except for a small mountain that rises from the landscape like an upturned bowl under a tablecloth. Small farming settlements surround this small, rural city.

The city gets its name from the Slavic word for "burned land" because of the way farmers cleared their land for planting and settlement. You can see just from the name that the people who settled it made their living from the rich earth. They raised crops and livestock, generation after generation.

In 1857, Frederick Ernst Schneider was born there, and there he lived until he was twenty-four and ready to make his own fortune.[8] When he left, dear ones engraved a pocket watch for him with "Görlitz, 1881," and sent him on his way.[9]

He traveled the Atlantic on a boat during the winter, arriving in 1882 in New York, as most European immigrants did then. Though that may seem like a miserable time to travel in a boat, it was wise to him. Having grown up in such a small, rural community, he was a farmer by birth and breeding, and he planned to farm in America. Landing in his new home in the winter would give him time to travel to his friends, establish himself, and gain farming work before the growing season.

From New York, Ernst came to the home of August Worms, a friend from Görlitz. August lived in Giddings, Texas, about a hundred miles northwest of Houston.[10] Giddings was in Lee County, named for Robert E. Lee, and the majority of people who lived there were displaced Southerners – wistful Confederates who were Anglo-Saxon in heritage.[11] But among them lived a community of Wends, a name for ethnically Slavic people living near German settlements and speaking German.[12] The Wends in Giddings even published a German-language newspaper.

Giddings must have seemed like a fortunate place to land for Ernst. He was in a mostly flat, very green place full of farms, just like Görlitz was. He could speak easily to the people around him, who had names like the people back home. Even the food in his adopted home would have been familiar German fare. Though he was in a new country among a new people, he could adjust to it gradually.

Ernst spoke not a word of English when he arrived. He learned from August and from another man in Giddings who wanted to learn German. Ernst taught the man German as he taught Ernst English. Once he was fluent, Ernst worked as a farmhand

16

in other communities, going up the Brazos River valley.

Here we can see the kind of adventurous spirit that drew Ernst over the ocean to America. Though he could have remained in the culturally familiar community in Giddings, Ernst took work in other towns, on other farms. He felt confident enough in his growing English skills to negotiate work for himself.

Over the next four years, he worked his way to Waco, which lay halfway between Dallas and San Antonio.[13] Occupying land formerly belonging to the Huaco Indians, Waco was a bustling town founded just a few decades before Ernst arrived. The suspension bridge the town built in 1873 made it a popular crossing spot for pioneers heading west, and its location near the Brazos River surrounded it with fertile farmland. Waco boasted a college, Baylor University. Right around the time Ernst lived there, Charles Alderton concocted the very first Dr. Pepper at Morrison's Old Corner Drug Store.[14]

Waco was prosperous and populous for a Western city of the time. It was the place to be for an unattached young man, strong and capable and looking for a bright future. And at Waco, Ernst found his future when he met Lizzie Bare.

Elizabeth Virginia Bare was only in Texas to visit her sister Maggie, who had just married Will Waite. The Bare girls were from Alderson, West Virginia.[15] Though the flat Texas landscape was very different from mountainous West Virginia, Alderson was split by a river, too, just like Waco. And many Texas newcomers were Southerners like Lizzie and her sister, Mag.

There were a host of reasons for Lizzie to feel at home in the place her sister had chosen, but Ernst became one of them. Though he was a farmhand, he kept his mustaches neatly trimmed and his hair short. He was a hard worker, a good provider, and an adventurous and determined man.

Lizzie and Ernst married November 7, 1886 in the First Methodist Church in Waco.[16] They posed for a wedding photo in their best things. Ernst leaned back in his chair, pleased and proud. Lizzie stood beside him with her hands on his chair; she was slim and straight, with a direct gaze. Neither forced a smile. They looked satisfied with their choice and eager to start their lives.

After their fall wedding, Lizzie and Ernst settled in Robinsonville, Texas, where they farmed for a year. Robinsonville was a suburb of Waco with its own school and post office.[17] There they had their first child, Anna Elizabeth, just over a year after their first anniversary.

But Mag and Will moved over two hundred miles northwest, to Iowa Park in Wichita County.[18] Family was precious, especially so far away from where the sisters had been born and raised. So after the growing season was over and the baby born, Lizzie and Ernst followed.

Lizzie took baby Anna first on the train and stayed with her sister. Then a cousin of Will's helped Ernst load up his wagon and follow with everything the couple owned. Despite being caught in a snowstorm in Jack County for days, Ernst arrived and looked over land with Will. Together, the two men purchased a 640-acre section four miles northeast of town. It was Tarrant County School land, and they got it for five dollars an acre and split it across the middle. Will and Mag got the south half, while Lizzie and Ernst took the north half.

Will and Ernst picked up rocks all over the county and built a rock house for the Schneiders. That rock house must have seemed a little out of the ordinary. After all, most settlers lived in dugouts until they could build a wood frame house.

But houses in Europe were mostly stone; maybe that small rock house was a tribute to Ernst's homeland as well as a symbol of the permanence he attached to the land he'd bought. After six years adrift, Ernst had purchased a piece of his new homeland and filled it with the family he'd created. A landowner and patriarch should live somewhere solid.

More children arrived at the rock house. Big sister Anna greeted a brother, Carl Watson, in 1889. After him, small Ula Bertha arrived in 1891, but she died a few short weeks later, right before Christmas. Two years later, in 1893, Ernst Earl joined the family, but tragedy struck the following summer when he died.

In 1895, Emma Ellen was born, and she lived and thrived, as did Fred Leonard, who arrived in 1898. The last child born to Ernst and Lizzie was Minnie Josephine, born in 1901. Anna was a big girl of thirteen when Minnie arrived, and Carl a strong boy of eleven.

Lizzie was a devout woman and a good mother, but she was not strong. Ernst improved the land he'd bought with a barn and silo and arable fields and a well close to the rock house, where it was convenient for Lizzie. But Ernst watched Lizzie anxiously, and in the summer of 1908, he started over and headed west, where he hoped that the drier prairie air would help to mend his wife's health.

Not even two years later, Lizzie took typhoid fever and died. Her oldest child was twenty-one; her youngest was nine. Ernst never remarried.

Frederick Ernst & Elizabeth Virginia Bare Schneider

CHAPTER THREE (3)
John Peter Kerlin &
Launa (Una) Lillian Thornton Kerlin

S AMUEL Dixon Thornton fought in the Civil War on the Confederate side, and that one fact about him shaped the rest of his life.[19]

Born in Missouri, Samuel was a US Army soldier. But towards the beginning of the Civil War, he got married and joined the Confederates. His family and he parted ways over his politics, and when his young wife died in childbirth, followed by the baby, he had no reason to go back to Missouri. Heartbroken, he kept fighting for the cause that had left him without home and family.

During the winter of 1864-1865, hungry and exhausted and cold in his threadbare uniform, he and two fellow soldiers arrived at a plantation in Louisiana and asked for shelter overnight. The owner, Andrew Brazzel, agreed, and his daughters took pity on the cold and hungry soldiers. They stayed up all night cutting material they had woven by hand and sewing it into coats to keep the soldiers warm.

Their good deed led to a happy ending for one of them. Samuel returned to Louisiana after the war, courted Laura Brazzel, and married her. Their romantic love story led to a happy marriage that produced seven children. The second youngest, Launa, was born in 1878 after the family moved to Texas. They moved to Crosby County in 1888, when Launa (nicknamed Una) was just ten years old.

One of their new neighbors was twenty-two year old John Peter Kerlin, an educated man who'd improved his homestead alone. He'd been one of the first settlers, filing on a homestead just eleven years after Hank Smith settled what would become Crosby County.

John was from Magnolia, Arkansas.[20] His father was a leather worker who made stirrups and holsters and belts and such for the Confederate Army until after the Civil War. After that, he made those things for the general public. He married and started a grand family – seven children.

But that thriving family lost its foundation when John was only eight years old. Everyone used guns in those days – they were tools to get you meat and rid you of pests as much as or more than weapons. People cleaned and loaded their own guns daily, and a lot of men even made their own bullets. John's father had a freak accident with his gun, and he died.

Left alone with seven children, one of whom was still an infant, John's mother did the best she could. But the children pitched in and helped her, too, as well as helping themselves. John worked hard and early, and he worked his way through school.

He loved education and was passionate about books. When he finished his own schooling, he got a certificate to teach. After teaching two terms, though, he decided that teaching wasn't for him. But for the rest of his life, he founded and directed and supported public schools.

John had an older brother named Jim who had settled in Texas. They hadn't seen each other in years, but they'd corresponded. Jim wrote John about the opportunities available for a strong, able man willing to work the land, and John joined him.

On March 12, 1888, John arrived on the train to meet his brother. He walked up and down the platform peering into the faces of strangers, but he didn't see his brother. Finally, he figured that there must have been some mistake. Maybe the letter with the date of his arrival had gone astray, or maybe something had happened to Jim to keep him from the station.

Either way, John figured that he may as well wait somewhere comfortable. He went into town for a drink and struck up a conversation with a stranger. John told the stranger who he was and who he'd come to meet.

"But I know Jim Kerlin," the stranger exclaimed. "In fact, I saw him in town not too long ago. You sit right here, and don't go anywhere. I'll fetch him for you."

Though John protested that he was sure he'd find his brother sooner or later and that the stranger didn't need to go to any trouble, the man insisted. So John let him go his way and stayed put, as the stranger had said.

Not much later, the stranger returned with a man John didn't recognize – his brother Jim. When they'd parted, John had been a young boy, and Jim had been a young man. Time had changed them both, and neither one recognized the other.

John stayed with Jim for a time while he looked at the land around. Parts of Arkansas were flat, but most of it was mountainous. Trees and boulders erupted in fields seemingly overnight. But here, every inch of Texas soil seemed ready to farm. You didn't have to pull up trees and root up rocks; you just had to turn over the sod.

Within two months, John had found the place to suit him: a piece of the Llano Estacado.[21] The only people who could be said to be neighbors were the Quakers who lived five miles away to the southwest, at Estacado. John filed on 640 acres, and he lived in a dugout lined with his wagon bed until he could afford a house.

It was a lonely life, breaking sod to plant crops and seeing no human face from one end of the day to another. But John was determined to make his place a profitable farm; so he kept at it from sunup to sundown, sleeping in the dugout at night and cooking over a campfire outside. Sometimes when he came home at night, he'd have to fling rattlesnakes out of his dugout before he could settle in.

While John was batching it, a younger brother from Arkansas came to visit him, bringing some treasured hound dogs. The two brothers cooked steaks for dinner over the campfire outside the dugout, and they used a long turning fork to rotate their steaks and keep them from burning. All the while, the hound dogs paced around the edge of the fire, salivating over the meat and drawing closer to dart in for a bite.

John's brother would take the turning fork from the meat, bop one of the hounds over the head, and go back to poking the steaks. John didn't like to say anything to a guest, but the practice put him off his dinner.

Guests were always welcome, though. And as John's nearest neighbors were the Quakers at Estacado, he saw them most often. Sometimes a group of solemn Quakers leading their even more solemn oxen would stop by John's dugout and invite him to cut cottonwood with them for winter fuel. They'd wait for John to hitch his mule team to his wagon runners, and they'd all go over the rim of the canyon to the river bottoms, where the cottonwood grew.

While John could only cut enough cottonwood at a time to fit on his wagon runners, the Quakers cut much more. They'd tie four or five wagon frames together, side by side, and hitch their oxen to this enormous contraption. As Quakers valued humility and hard work and open-hearted sharing, they expected their animals to live by their values. And Quakers were taught from youth never to avenge themselves but to give place to wrath, as Paul taught the Romans; so they learned to be kind to people and animals and to speak gently to them.

One time when John followed the Quakers to cut cottonwood, he saw that the Quakers' lead oxen had had about enough of hard work and humility and was ready for some rest and relaxation instead. The Quakers were, too, after the strenuous labor of cutting winter fuel. But the Quakers knew that they must go back up the canyon and across the plains home before they could rest; the oxen didn't.

The Quaker elder approached the lead ox and spoke kindly to him. "I know that thou art tired, friend, but food and rest await thee at home. Thou cannot stay here and be cared for. Get up now, friend, and take up thy labors. Thou will be rewarded when they are finished."

Surprisingly enough, the ox was not persuaded.

Next the elder tried reading the Bible to his tired beast, and then laying hands on the animal and praying. But the ox proved as resistant to scripture and prayer as it had to reason. The elder was at the end of his rope. So he went to the other end of the ox.

In the same quiet, gentle tone he had used three times before, the elder said, "I'll not beat thee, and I'll not curse thee. But I surely will twist thy tail off." After about forty cranks of its tail, the ox moved.

John worked hard and saved carefully, and eventually he bought a house and had it moved to his land. He paid forty dollars and an iron skillet for it. It may seem odd to go to the trouble of moving an already built house onto land you own, especially considering how good those early pioneers were at living off the land and making what they needed for themselves.

But nearly all the wood you could find on the plains was slender cottonwood and scrubby mesquite. Neither was sturdy enough for house-building. In fact, that lack of tall trees led the first European and American explorers of the Great Plains to label them the Great American Desert. If trees couldn't grow on the plains, reasoned the explorers, then neither could anything else of value.[22]

The lack of tall trees was one reason why Texas settlement followed the railroads. As soon as another track was laid closer to the western edge of the frontier, farmers could buy the wood it hauled for houses and barns and fences. And those improvements, built as they were of that scarce and precious wood, demanded care – especially against the dreaded prairie fire.

Cowboy and Indian movies would have you believe that the greatest danger to a Texas settler was a band of Apache on the warpath. But John Kerlin only saw a Native American raiding party once, several miles off. What really struck fear into the heart of a settler was a roaring prairie fire, sweeping across the plains as fast as a trotting horse.

That kind of fire could devour every expensive improvement, all the work and savings of years, in a matter of minutes. And there was no way to stop one just with water drawn from wells. The fire would stop if it reached wide water that quenched it or a wide strip of earth that starved it. But as long as it met grass, it spread.

As you could see so far into the distance on those flat plains, you'd have warning that a fire was coming. And if a neighbor in between you and the fire could stop it at his place, that was all the better for you. So you'd hitch a plow to your mule and race to help him plow a firebreak. If that fire was coming straight for you, you'd plow as fast as you could, all around your improvements.

John knew of two cowboys who saw a fire coming. Cowboys didn't cultivate fields; so they didn't have a plow handy. What they did have was cattle. So they killed a steer and dragged the carcass around and around their campsite to kill the grass and tear it up and save them from the fire.

Some of those improvements the early settlers built were schools. Two years after John Kerlin moved to the prairie, he and the other settlers of Crosby County counted noses and found that there were enough children present to form a school district. As John was the only man qualified to serve as trustee, he did, though he had no children at the time. He ended up serving as trustee, hiring teachers and supervising the school, for over twenty-five years.

S.D. Thornton and John Kerlin remained close neighbors, visiting back and forth, for years. When they met, Una was a child. But she grew up. And in those days, when the population was so scarce, nothing was more natural than to marry close – to marry a neighbor you knew and trusted and had had a chance to watch for years. In Una's case, she married someone who'd sat around her dinner table, someone she'd seen handle hardship and responsibility well and with good humor.

John and Una decided to marry when Una was seventeen. They offered to wait, if S.D. wanted to send Una to further schooling, but he didn't. He was probably happy for his young daughter to settle close by, close enough to visit once in a while as her new husband had all those years.

After the marriage in 1895, John and Una had a daughter in 1896. They named her Laura after Una's mother, the plantation owner's daughter. Soon Mae and Bernice joined their sister.

As John Kerlin's family grew, so did his responsibility in the community. In addition to acting as school trustee, he became deacon of the Baptist church and justice of the peace. But John didn't just sit in some town office and administrate from behind a desk. No – he was still a working farmer plowing fields and planting crops and tending animals.

Once, while he was out in his fields plowing with the mule, John welcomed a couple riding in to see him. They wanted to be married; in fact, they had a marriage certificate in hand, ready for him to sign. A witness to the marriage was necessary, and luckily for them, Una Kerlin was already on her way out to the field to bring her husband a cool drink.

John performed the marriage, and Una witnessed it. Then the couple went their way, while John resumed plowing and Una returned to the house.

She had almost reached home when she looked at the certificate she held. Maybe she thought fondly of her own wedding day, or maybe she wanted to remember the names of the sweet couple, or maybe she looked idly at the paper in her hand for want of much else to see but grassy plain. Either way, she saw immediately that the marriage certificate was made out for the wrong county.

The marriage John had just performed was illegal; that couple wasn't married at all.

Una ran across the fields to catch John and explain. And as soon as John understood what had happened, he unhitched his mule from the plow, hopped astride him, took the offending certificate from Una, and rode as fast as the mule would go to catch the couple. He returned after dark, having caught the erstwhile newlyweds after a hard afternoon and evening riding, determined to read very carefully any future license he signed.

Besides overseeing the schools and the Baptists and the minor legal problems of the county, John helped move the Singer store to Lubbock. New stores were good for commerce and growth, and John wasn't afraid to get his hands dirty. Considering the vast spaces common to pioneers, Lubbock wasn't too far away – he'd probably trade with the owner.

That Singer store grew, and so did the town of Lubbock. Though the site is now the center of a busy, fully developed downtown, when John moved the Singer store, it stood aloof from any neighbors. And chickens scratched in the back yard.

Meanwhile, Una was busy raising the girls. Like all pioneer women in those days, she kept a garden and preserved what she grew. She made clothes and washed and mended them. She cooked meals and washed dishes and kept herself and her children and her house neat and presentable.

Una also helped with births. There were no hospitals nearby, and doctors were scarce as well. Women helped one another in those days, and between relatives and neighbors and church family, some older woman was generally available to help some younger woman when her time to deliver came. Like all other talents, some older women were more suited to healing than others. Una must have had a calming presence and a gentle touch and some practical knowledge, because women sent for her.[23]

In 1907, when Una was twenty-nine, she discovered that her turn to need a midwife was coming again.[24] She was due in the fall. Elated at his growing family and able to afford the expense, John hauled wood from Amarillo, over a hundred miles to the north. And then he built an eight-room house, huge by prairie standards, to hold his dearest treasures – his girls.

But on August 10, a fire destroyed the house. Luckily, all the family escaped safely. But the huge new house and most of what it had held was gone. John and Una had to start over.

They were fortunate that their nearest neighbor was family. The Kerlins moved in with the Thorntons while John again hauled wood from Amarillo to build another house. This time, the house was four rooms. And the Kerlins brought baby Iris to it when it was finished.

To Laura Kerlin, a girl of eleven, the new sister must have seemed her own special child, in a way. At the time of Iris's birth, Laura was old enough to look forward to life as a wife and a mother, and oldest girls are always special helpers to their mothers. So the oldest Kerlin daughter and the youngest shared a sweet bond.

There is a photo of the Kerlins taken when Iris was still small. The family sits on a blanket outside, as if they're enjoying a picnic. Between and around proud papa John and sweet mother Una sit and stand Laura, Mae, Bernice, and Iris. They wear dresses their mother made, and their hair is done in large, old-fashioned bows. Despite the plain expressions forced by the first cameras, you can see their ease with one another and their genuine affection for each other.

Around the time of that photo, in 1908, the Schneider family moved to Crosby County. Laura Kerlin and Carl Schneider, close to the same age, grew up as friends and neighbors. They saw one another at church and school and community events.

When Carl lost his mother, Lizzie, Una was likely one of the neighbors who brought food to the Schneider house and sang hymns at the funeral. Neighbors shared bonds and memories like these that no one outside the community ever could. It was a powerful draw to marry and have families close by, where the people you joined knew and remembered and loved the people who had been dear to you.

Life was rich and full for the Kerlins. They worked hard and enjoyed the fruits of their labor. They contributed their time and their knowledge and their devotion to making the small community of Farmer a place of safety and abundance and learning. Their girls went to school in Farmer, and when she was old enough, Laura went away to school.

But she didn't have to worry too much about missing home. [25] Una wrote her lively letters all about what was happening, from new babies born to how the garden was doing to news about the neighbors. Mother and daughter were as close as ever.

John Peter Kerlin & Launa (Una) Thornton Kerlin

CHAPTER FOUR (4)
Carl Watson Schneider &
Laura Kerlin Schneider

CARL's earliest memories took place in Iowa Park, in the rock house and in the fields and creeks around it.[26] Lizzie was friends with a woman named Mrs. Lowrance, who had a son named Gale. Carl was fast friends with Gale. They hunted coons and pulled pranks (like stealing Gale's older brother Lock's clothes while he swam) and generally just enjoyed one another's company.

Once they got into a fight, and their mothers made them kiss to make up. Gale told Carl he'd rather have had a spanking than have to kiss him, and Carl agreed. But they sure didn't fight again, at least not where their mothers could see.

Iowa Park was becoming a settled place when Carl was young. There were enough people in the small town to support real celebrations, with fireworks and speeches and lemonade that cost five cents a glass. After one May Day picnic, the lemonade vendor slashed his prices and offered all the lemonade you could drink for five cents. Carl drank two glasses and quit, but Gale downed seven or eight glasses. They didn't stay down long.

From an early age, Carl worked hard with his father whenever he wasn't in school. For a long time, until Fred was born, Carl was his father's only son, and Ernst grew to rely on Carl. Ernst had a fanning mill for cleaning grain, a grind rock for sharpening farm tools, and a corn sheller for turning ears of corn into feed, and Carl learned to turn them all.

Raising grain drew pests, like the squirrels that would break into the corn crib down by the creek and carry ears of corn off by the shucks. And of course, the creek itself drew and bred mosquitoes, which got into the eyes and noses and mouths of cow and milker alike on the farm. They were so bad in rainy years that Ernst built fires in the middle of the cow pen to drive the mosquitoes away with the smoke.

And of course, where there are cows, there will be cow pies, and where there are cow pies, there will be flies. Such is life for a farmer.

Ernst raised wheat and oats and corn and occasional cotton, and Carl saw the first threshers running on horsepower – horses harnessed to crossed bars and walking in a circle like a carousel. Wheat poured from a chute like a fountain of gold. That technology was revolutionary for farmers who employed methods that hadn't changed much since biblical times.

Carl also saw the first cotton gins taking over the work that slaves and poor farmers had done before by removing the cotton fibers from the seed. The usable cotton was pressed by firm hand and stomping foot into bales. Machines were changing the way farmers farmed – slowly.

A neighbor got a mechanical cultivator, one a mule could pull and the farmer could ride. When Ernst and Lizzie saw it, they remarked that they'd be ashamed to make the mule pull the machine and them, too. You have to wonder what they'd think of the metal monsters crawling over modern farmland.

Lizzie was frightened when she saw the first cars zooming along the narrow Texas roads. She told Carl and Anna, "If you see an automobile coming while you're riding to school, jump off the horse and let him go, and you get right under the fence!"

While Ernst and Carl worked hard in the fields raising wheat and oats and corn, Lizzie worked hard keeping the rock house neat and full of good food and happy children. Carl helped inside only occasionally. The first time he ever dried dishes with Anna, he was pressed into service because Lizzie was away acting as a midwife.

In pioneer days, you came when a neighbor needed you; you did whatever you could to help. Once Lizzie helped some neighbors, the McCalls, by taking in their boy when the family was taking a trip. Having him to stay was a true sacrifice, because his feet stank. You could hardly stay in the house when he pulled his shoes off.

Not knowing how to broach the subject with a guest, Lizzie worked by subterfuge. One night Lizzie said, "Carl, I wish you'd go and wash your feet. They stink so badly!" Carl looked up at her, surprised, as she'd never made that criticism before. Soon afterwards, the McCall boy went up to bed, and Lizzie explained that the false criticism was a hint.

The McCall boy didn't take it. Fortunately, he wasn't a permanent resident of the rock house.

One guest who stayed longer was Lizzie's father, Jacob Bare. He came one day to visit his daughters, Lizzie and Mag, and he stayed for a year. He was the only grandparent that Carl ever met. Carl never laid eyes on Grandmother Bare, and Ernst's parents in Germany might as well have been on the moon.

Of course, the Waites were close by, on the other half of the land Ernst and Will had bought together. It was an easy thing to run over to Aunt Mag and Uncle Will's house for a shared meal or to play with a cousin or to trade work. At least, it was until they moved in 1900, when Carl was eleven. Then there were new neighbors, strangers where there had been family.

Neighbors all around in Iowa Park came to be a sort of extended family to the Schneiders in the rock house. Like other pioneers, they knew the truth of the Proverb, "Better is a neighbor that is near than a brother far off."[27] There were neighbors down the creek, Mr. and Mrs. Corridon, that Carl called Grandpa and Grandma.

And some of the Schneider's neighbors in Iowa Park were German friends who would come to eat and stay all day Sunday after services. The adults would eat, and then the mothers would clear and reset the table for the kids. Carl remembered feeling half starved by the time he got a turn to eat.

But closer than this extended family was the little family inside the rock house, and after years of sorrow and disappointment, it began to grow again. Carl must have rejoiced when his brother Fred was born. Here at last was a co-laborer in the making to share the work with him!

Unfortunately, Fred seemed prone to accident. Once he fell backward in his high chair and hit his head on the hard rock wall, opening a nasty gash. Another time, he fell face first into an apple barrel and cut his head on a nail. And then there was the time when he slid off a haystack and sliced his head on an old plow point.

Fred survived, though, much to the relief and gladness of his family. He grew strong, though he wasn't able to help in the fields until Carl was sixteen. For most of his childhood Carl was the main help for farm work and running errands.[28]

Some of the errands he ran were to Lizzie's butter and egg customers in and around Iowa Park on Saturday mornings. Ernst built a box with shelves and a lid to hold the butter, and to keep the butter fresh, Lizzie wrapped her butter in cloths cool and wet from the spring. Carl made the deliveries in good time, before the heat of the day, and then he'd conduct any other business Ernst had for him in town.

Once Ernst sent Carl to the blacksmith on a Saturday morning after Lizzie's deliveries. Carl went barefoot most of the time, as most farm boys did – a practice that didn't bother them as they walked through soft earth. On this day, however, Carl learned why blacksmiths didn't go barefoot. He stepped on a piece of hot metal and burned the fool out of his feet. Luckily, he had Lizzie's cool, wet butter cloths to wrap his feet until he could get home in the wagon.

Survival as a pioneer depended on taking advantage of every resource you could find. In early summer, Carl picked tubs full of plums from the wild trees lining the Red River. Lizzie could dry them for prunes, stew them into jellies and preserves, and can them whole to use later for pies or cakes or a treat after dinner.[29]

On hot summer days, Ernst would take Carl with the horses hitched to the running gear of the wagon and go down to the river bottoms to cut cottonwood. Together, the father and son loaded the trunks and big branches on the running gear until they had all that the horses could carry. That wood was worth fifty cents a load in town.

In late summer, when heat shimmered over the land, Ernst and Carl cut hay north of Iowa Park near Burnett Ranch. In early days, Ernst had cut that hay alone and sold it to the ranch to feed their stock through the winter. Now he and Carl cut it for the use of their own animals.

The summer before Carl was fourteen, he got a job at the thresher, cleaning up in front of the separator. It was the hottest and dirtiest job at the harvest, but Carl earned a man's wages for it: $1.50 a day and board. He used the money for his first store-bought suit.[30]

Once the fields were harvested and the work of gathering and putting by done, Carl and Gale Lowrance hunted coons by the creeks. Carl had two small shepherd dogs that helped him track the animals. Raccoon hides were valuable, with their distinctive ringed tails, and the boys skinned the raccoons they caught and sold the pelts.

During the fall and winter and early spring, Carl and his brother and sisters went to school. As more and more children grew old enough to go, Ernst upgraded them from walking to horseback to a cart to a buggy. But in 1906 when Carl was seventeen, his early schooling came to an end when the county changed his school district at the same time that Anna got her teacher's certificate.

There was plenty for him to do on the farm, though. Ernst saved enough to buy a larger house in town, and during the winter, he sent his family to live in Iowa Park. Then Ernst moved that house to his land and tore down the old rock house the Schneiders had outgrown. He built new rooms to add to the new house, and he dug a well close to the house for Lizzie's convenience.

Carl had to draw water from that well to give the stock in dry weather. His hands blistered from hauling the bucket up and down on its rope so many times.

Despite the many improvements Ernst Schneider made to his land, he knew that he couldn't stay there. Lizzie was not well. Based on the fact that Ernst moved his family to the dry, windy air of the high plains, famous among sufferers of lung conditions for its curative powers, Lizzie may have had some kind of illness or damage to her lungs.[31]

When the Schneiders moved west in 1908, Carl was eighteen. The family packed a covered wagon and a buggy, and what would not fit in them they stored in the granary. On August 20, 1908, the family rode west, stopping at settlements and towns along the way to see what kind of land was available and what the air was like.[32]

Lizzie and little Minnie rode in the buggy. Ernst, Anna, Carl, Emma, and Fred rode on the wagon. On the way out of town, they stopped by the Lowrance farm to say goodbye. It must have been a hard parting; the families were close friends.

The Schneiders drove ten or fifteen miles out of town to see Mr. Sterns at Beaver Creek. The Sterns were old friends who hosted the Schneider family for several days. Here there was another round of goodbyes.

The family went around thirty miles to Vernon from there. When Carl entered Vernon, Texas, forty-one miles northwest of Iowa Park, it was as far as he had ever traveled from home.

He was at the edge of the map of his life. He could have written, as ancient mapmakers did for uncharted seas: *here, there be monsters.* He had no idea what to expect.

Ernst took the journey slowly, out of consideration for Lizzie. In those days there were wagon yards where travelers could camp. Every wagon yard had a bunk house and a cook stove where people could sleep and prepare their own food with the materials in their chuck boxes: meal, flour, salt, beans, dried or smoked meat, and pots and pans. Where there was no wagon yard, they camped on the land.

Before they came to the Caprock, the Schneiders looked at land in Crowell, Paducah, and Dickens City, where a ranch was trying to start a town called Espuila – a town which was later swallowed by the town of Spur. Between twenty and sixty miles lay between the places Carl remembered. If the family traveled twenty miles a day, they would need ten days to cover the nearly two hundred miles between Iowa Park and old Emma. If they stopped several days in between to let Lizzie rest, September would be well underway before they stopped.

You have to wonder what they thought and how they felt on that final leg of the journey. Here they'd been chasing good air and good land, and before them rose the red wall of the Caprock Escarpment – the same divine palisade that had inspired the conquistadors.

Carl remembered that it was a bad hill. Despite the fact that the wagon had good brakes, Carl and the other children walked behind the wagon and put rocks behind the wheels to keep it from rolling backwards. There had been another bad hill earlier, approaching Dickens City. People had warned them about it, and the children had to put rocks behind the wheels there, too.

But Ernst kept climbing those bad hills despite the warnings. Maybe he figured that you had to climb the bad hills to get to the good air. And when he stopped his wagon at the top of that last bad hill just outside old Emma, he must have seen that there were no more bad hills to climb. He was as high as he could go. And the air up there blew dry and fast. It was just the place to heal a pair of swampy lungs.

The Schneiders camped in the wagon yard at old Emma, a yard owned by a land agent.[33] The man took Ernst Schneider to the Farmer community and showed him the land there. It was just what Ernst had imagined when he'd left Iowa Park. He bought a half section.

The Schneiders' land bordered the Wrights' land. Mr. Wright generously hosted the family until Ernst could get shelter built for his family. He had to haul lumber from Plainview, which was a three-day journey, including loading time. But soon, Ernst had a shed and granary built on his new land. It wasn't a house, but it was enough. And he had a well drilled near it, first thing.

Then he left to retrieve the belongings he had stored in the granary of the old farm in Iowa Park. He went by way of the railroad in Plainview.

A few days after he left, a prairie fire fed by dead grass and high winds started close to the New Mexico border and headed right for the small community of Farmer, and the new Schneider farm. Generous new neighbors came to the rescue. Paul Payne saw the fire coming and hurried to the Schneider farm with four mules and a disk plow; he plowed circles all around the new shed and granary and well. Other men hurried to help the newest citizens of Farmer, too. Together, they stopped the fire at the road running north to south through the Schneider land.

Ernst shipped the family's belongings to Plainview. Carl, Mr. Wright, Mr. Junious Payne and others took five wagons to meet the train. They unloaded Ernst's boxcar and drove his possessions to his farm.

Once the family's belongings were on their land, it was time to fence Ernst's half section. This far west, the land was still in transition from free-range ranch land to farmland, and it behooved any responsible farmer to make sure that no marauding cattle could lunch on his crop.

Fencing the land was a tough job, and so Mr. Wright helped Ernst and Carl. Carl and Mr. Wright dug the post holes, while Ernst set the poles and fixed braces. Then all three men ran the wire and stretched it.

A half section is 320 acres, an area of land with a perimeter of 4,551.91 meters, or nearly 14,935 feet. If you figure for a post hole every six feet, you get about 2,489 post holes. At around two feet per post hole, that's 4,978 feet – nearly a mile down if you stacked all the holes on top of one another.

That's a lot of digging.

They finished before it was time to plant in the spring of 1909, and they planted and tended and harvested the crop for that year. Ernst built a house. Over that season and the next, Carl broke most of 190 acres with a walking sod plow.

Meanwhile, everyone watched Lizzie for signs that the healthy air of the high plains was doing her good.

But in the spring of 1910, typhoid fever swept the family, striking Lizzie, Anna, and Emma. Anna and Emma survived. Their mother did not. She died in the early summer, when sod crops waved in the fields.[34] It was a dry year.

Ernst could spare Carl, and home must have been a different place without his mother. The same neighbors that had saved the farm from fire and moved everything from the boxcar at Plainview probably cared for the family in its sickness and loss. Carl might have felt out of place around so many strange and well-meaning women.

So Carl went to look for work at Crowell with two other friends. They found a place with a cotton farmer who wanted choppers – boys who would go up and down the rows in the punishing heat and chop weeds out of the cotton stalks.

The normal arrangement was a wage plus room and board. But this farmer was a bachelor who let them know that he didn't intend to cook for them. Carl volunteered to cook for everyone. That meant less chopping for him, and he was all right with that arrangement.

Carl's friends started chopping right away while Carl went with the farmer to buy supplies: beans, potatoes, meat, flour, and yeast cakes. Carl cooked in the morning and chopped cotton in the afternoon. When the fields were done, the farmer said that he sure hated to go back to his own cooking.

Though his two friends went home after they finished working for the cotton farmer in Crowell, Carl wasn't ready to go home yet. He went to Chillicothe, where an old Iowa Park neighbor, a hardware store owner named McPherson, got him work on the wheat harvest. The wheat harvest would have lasted into September – two years to the month since he'd arrived on the plains. He stayed a few days with his Aunt Mag and then went home.

It has been said that the cure for any grief is salt water: sweat, tears, or the sea.[35] Carl chose sweat. And alone in all those golden waves, who was there to see any tears?

The taste of independence did him more good than just healing his grief. He was retracing his father's journey as a young man: an epic migration followed by work as a hired hand on other men's farms. After a winter at home, a winter he probably spent doing chores like caring for animals and mending fences, Carl put in his father's crop again.

1911 was another dry year, and the meager crop looked as if it would burn to death in the fields. This time another kind of necessity than grief drove Carl to look for work. He and his friend Willis Wright went to Wellington, Kansas, to hire as laborers for the wheat harvest.

When they showed up to the farm that wanted work, the farmer could only hire one boy. Carl urged Willis to take the job, and he found work at another farm. They agreed to meet at the depot on Sundays. Willis made it to the first Sunday meeting, but by the second he had gone home. It was hot and dry in Kansas, too.

The dry summer weather broke in July, and rain fell back home in Farmer. By the time Carl finished working the Kansas wheat harvest and came home in August, Ernst's row crops were doing all right.

That September, Carl turned twenty-one. Back then, twenty-one was the voting age. Carl was a man and a full citizen who could buy property of his own, enter a legal contract, or marry. He wasn't ready to do any of those things, but he was ready to think more about his future.

Carl spent the next year helping Ernst around the farm, building a concrete storage tank and watering trough. He hauled sand from the canyon southeast of Cone and from Floyd County, twelve miles south of Lockney, and then he and Ernst and Lester Cowan mixed the concrete for those tanks.

During this time, Ernst raised a little cotton, and when it was time for harvest, it was Carl's job to take the cotton bolls to the gin to remove the seed and press the fibers into bales. Seventeen miles away in Lorenzo, the only gin available was busy, as most farmers harvested around the same time; so Carl employed various stratagems to avoid the wait. Sometimes he'd sleep at the gin, pulling the wagon cover over him, so that he'd be first in line when the gin opened. Sometimes he'd sleep early at the farm, rising around midnight to make the drive.

Carl also helped a Farmer family, the Englishes, move cattle from their farm to a ranch south of the Half Circle Ranch. He helped them brand cattle, too. They enlarged their herd several times by buying from neighbors, and Carl helped Orville English move these animals from their former homes to the English ranch. For all intents and purposes, he was a cowboy.

Once Carl drove cattle from Cone to Crosbyton, arriving in the dark of a moonless night. A yearling calf ran off on its own down a side lane, and as the nearest, Carl chased him, though he could barely see in the dark. Suddenly a barbed wire fence appeared in the way. Though the calf saw it in time to jump, Carl's horse whirled and slid against it, scraping his side, tearing Carl's boot, and scraping Carl's foot badly.

The foot healed, and Carl went back to work on the farm. But he hadn't stopped wondering about his future. In the fall of 1912, Carl enrolled in Metropolitan Business College in Dallas, Texas. He stayed there for two academic years until the spring of 1914, working in town between terms.[36]

But then Carl took measles, and he ran out of money – two excellent reasons to come home. He recuperated from his illness and slid back into the routine of work on the farm: plant, tend, harvest, and all the while care for the animals that did the farm work and were used as food.

In 1915 when she was twenty-eight, Anna married John Albert Ragle. The couple moved to Lovington, New Mexico. And then in 1916, Emma married Orville English, the neighbor Carl had helped herd cows. Those two older girls had been housekeepers to Ernst and substitute mothers to Minnie, who had been barely nine when Lizzie died.

Living rough with a busy dad and two older brothers didn't seem like the kind of atmosphere Minnie needed. So before Emma's wedding, Ernst loaded fourteen-year-old Minnie with all her worldly goods in a covered wagon and took her to Anna and Albert's house in New Mexico to live. Ernst was gone three weeks.

Ernst and Carl and Fred lived alone that year, tending to the work of the farm and eating their own cooking. It must have been strange being three men alone where first Lizzie and then Lizzie's daughters had kept house. It must have felt lonely without Minnie's girlish laughter to lighten the evenings after the last cow had been milked and the last tool put away.

In 1917, Ernst determined to bring his youngest daughter a little closer. Carl persuaded him to buy a 1914 Ford car to make the journey in one day instead of spending weeks in the covered wagon. Ernst agreed, and the trip to get Minnie took a day on the dirt roads. But the car became Carl's sole property – Ernst preferred his buggy and wouldn't learn to drive.

Minnie lived for the 1917-1918 school year in Floydada,

nearly twenty miles north of Farmer. That was close enough to run up and see her from time to time and to bring her home for holidays. Of course, the men were still batching it: Carl cooked, Fred milked, and Ernst did the feeding. All three worked in the fields.

During the time that the Schneider siblings were marrying and leaving, the world was at war. Ernst must have felt sad that his old country was torn and troubled so. But he must have felt worse in 1917 when his new country took up arms against the place he had been born. He could not have shared this conflict in his heart with his oldest son, though, for Carl went into the Army on August 12, 1918, just a month shy of his twenty-ninth birthday.

Sixty men from Ralls County journeyed together to San Antonio to join up. Little did they know that they would have to fight a deadlier enemy than the Triple Alliance. They would have to fight the Spanish Influenza.

Carl caught the flu in San Antonio and went to the Army hospital there. At least one soldier died every night. He must have wondered, as the lifeless bodies left one by one, whether he would survive long enough to don a uniform.

He did.

There is a picture of him in uniform. Farm work had built his muscles and grown him tall and strong, but illness hollowed his cheeks and the flesh around his eyes. He looked gaunt and serious and determined. But that's not how he sounded in his letters to his neighbor, Laura Kerlin.

To Laura, the Caprock Escarpment wasn't an intimidating frontier. It wasn't wild land. It was just where she grew up. Her parents and grandparents had been pioneers, and she lived on settled land, thanks to them.

Laura and her sisters Mae and Bernice grew up close in age. When Laura was eleven, baby Iris joined the family, and Laura became a kind of second mother to her. Life for Laura consisted of school and homework and housework on the farm. Una taught her to garden and to can, to cook and to clean, to sew and to quilt, and to raise animals and to butcher them.

Laura's father, John Kerlin, was the trustee for the county schools, and Laura inherited from him a great love of books and of the knowledge that could be found in them. She liked and understood poetry, and she committed much of it to memory. She knew poems for nearly any occasion that might arise.[37]

She and Carl attended the same church in Farmer, though they did not attend the same school. Laura was almost seven years younger than Carl, who had left his schooldays behind in Iowa Park. Laura had been twelve in 1908, when a nearly nineteen-year-old Carl had arrived in Farmer. Her schoolmate was Carl's younger sister, Emma.

The one church in Farmer served Methodists and Baptists alike. Preachers from both denominations circulated once a month through the Farmer pulpit, and officials from either denomination took turns ordering Sunday school literature, one year Baptist and the next, Methodist.[38]

Carl and Laura also would have gathered at the same community events, like First Friday Nights. On the first Friday of each month, the scattered neighborhood of farmers flocked to the building in town that housed both church and school, amusing themselves and each other with ice cream suppers, stories, dances, and other programs.

Laura had an independent spirit and a desire to see something of the world. Anyone looking at her red hair might see a clue to the fire and determination within her. When Laura finished school, she didn't want to settle down. She got her state teaching certificate instead.

When she finished, she began teaching school. As involved as John Kerlin had been in the Crosby County schools, teaching must have seemed second nature to the studious girl. She taught at several different schools, and Una reported to her when she left one that all the children missed "Miss Laura."

Una also hinted that Carl Schneider had hated to leave without seeing her again. There was another boy, one whom Una did not deign to name, who wanted to see her, too. But Una warned that he was the kind to make a woman think that she ought to be grateful for the honor of marrying him and being allowed to provide cooking and housekeeping services for him. Una wanted much better for her daughter than marrying proud Pat Leigh.

Laura went on hunting trips with her Uncle Tom, and she stayed for a while in Louisiana, where Una's mother Laura had lived before her handsome Confederate soldier had come for her. In September 1919, letters addressed to Laura Kerlin found her at the Service Motor Truck Company of Monroe, Louisiana, where she boarded. A month later, she and Mae were a hundred miles west at Draughon's Business College in Shreveport, Louisiana.

Una wrote letters to Laura of the news back home. Someone named Delmer dropped off a child named Delia to stay while Una was away from home. Una came home to find the small girl with her winter things on the front porch, and stories about her lively tongue and raging moods interrupt the news of crops and canning and sewing and cleaning.

From school, Laura must have laughed over her perplexed mother parenting this tempestuous, motherless waif. Maybe she was glad her mother had such a warm and affectionate distraction from the hard things of life, like the baby Una had helped deliver who died.

Laura got other letters. Emma Schneider English wrote of her darling baby Ruth, while Iris wrote about school and her clothes and funny Delia. Carl Schneider wrote of town happenings – parties and harvests and his work on the farm. Cousins and friends wrote of romances and suspected romances and social events. Everyone wrote of how much Laura was loved and missed.

But Laura didn't stay away as long as she had planned. One moment Una was writing newsy, affectionate letters about cleaning house and tending the recalcitrant Delia and a small problem the doctor was going to examine and the happenings in Farmer, and the next, Emma Schneider English was sending her condolences over Una's passing.

Una died on December 8, 1919. Laura and Mae came home to keep house for their father, mourn their mother, and care for their small sister Iris, who was only twelve. Iris needed a mother, and since Una was gone, Laura would be that tender mother while Iris needed her.

Una had mentioned that Delmer was thinking of sending Delia to his sister in Oklahoma. Maybe he did; she wasn't mentioned again. The Kerlins would have had as much as they could do to care for Iris after generous, hard-working Una died.

After Una Kerlin died, John Kerlin divided his land. He kept half for himself, and he divided the other half into four equal shares, giving one to each daughter. Laura had eighty acres free and clear in her own name.

Carl and Laura were in the same boat. Both lived with widower fathers, and both helped to care for vulnerable younger sisters. Both had, in a way, put their own lives on hold to support grieving families. Both set examples of selfless compassion.

Discharged from the Army after serving a stint in the balloon corps at Fort Sill, Oklahoma, Carl returned home in April of 1919. He and Laura again began moving in the same small circles in Farmer – Carl as a bachelor farmer and Laura as a single schoolteacher.

But in the fall of 1920, Laura went to West Texas State Normal School in Canyon, Texas, more than a hundred miles north of Farmer. She came home for vacations, and she set aside time between school and work to sew Iris the dresses she needed. She stayed for two years.

She didn't go for the full four years she'd need for a bachelor of arts. Maybe her father needed her at home. Maybe she ran out of money for school. Maybe Mae and Bernice needed a chance to learn away from home, and Laura wanted to give them that chance. For whatever reason, she came home in the spring of 1922 and taught school again in the fall, and she looked after Iris and the farmhouse.

In 1922, Fred Schneider got married and moved away – first to Kansas and later to California. Minnie was grown now, twenty-one years old, and no one needed to look after her anymore. She could help take care of the farm. As Ernst had some extra room and could use an extra hand on the farm, he invited his half-brother, Gustav Seidel, to stay with him and work.

51

Gustav had followed Ernst to America a few years after Ernst made the trip, but Gustav went to Searcy County, Arkansas. In Arkansas, Gustav married and had two children: Rose Anna and Andrew. Sadly, Gustav's wife died while the children were small, and their grandmother and an uncle helped to raise them.

Once his children were grown and gone, Gustav was free to live elsewhere; so he came to Texas with Ernst. And Ernst needed help on the farm for another reason than Fred's absence. Ernst had facial cancer, and he needed to leave for treatments in Joplin, Missouri from time to time. Even with Fred gone and Ernst ill, Carl and Gustav could keep the farm going.

Tragically, Gustav met with an accident. While Ernst was gone for cancer treatment and Carl was away from the farm, Gustav took Carl's team of mules out to the fields to do some disking. The team ran away, and Gustav was caught under the disk plow. Ernst buried him in the cemetery at Cone; his children were unable to come to the funeral.

Life continued for Carl and for Laura. Seed-time and harvest came and passed and came and passed again. Carl farmed while Laura taught school and kept house. They saw each other often.

In 1925, Ernst moved to Crosbyton with Minnie, who was twenty-four, and Emma, who was thirty. Emma brought her small daughter, Ruth, but her husband Orville stayed on their ranch and came for visits when he could. Ernst was quite ill, and his daughters cared for him and took him to treatments.

When he could, Carl helped them. He drove to Crosbyton, sat up all night with his father so that his sisters could rest, and then drove back the next morning early. Then he'd work all the next day on the farm. He was in sole charge of the farm and all the work on it. He cooked and cleaned for himself. But he must have had a little time to visit with his pretty neighbor, Laura.

January 17, 1926 was a Sunday. Carl and Laura drove together to the Baptist parsonage in Ralls with license in hand and were married there by Elmer Kelly. The short ceremony made the minister, who preached in Farmer once a month, late to church. He apologized for his tardiness by telling the congregation that he'd had to perform a wedding. The congregation then looked around and counted noses and figured out that Carl and Laura were the happy couple.

After the ceremony, Carl and Laura went to Emma and Orville's ranch to stay. Then they headed to Plainview, where they bought a complete housekeeping outfit to be sent after them to the Schneider farm. From Plainview, they traveled to Mag and Will Waite's farm, and then they went to Anna and Albert's house in Olton, Texas (they'd moved from New Mexico). It is plain from the route that Carl was eager to show off his new bride to the relatives that didn't live in Farmer and didn't already know how wonderful Laura was.

One of the realities of getting married in the winter was the risk of snowstorm. It snowed so hard the week after the wedding that the Plainview store couldn't deliver the housekeeping supplies until things calmed down.

But then Carl and Laura settled into married life on the Schneider property, all on their own. They lived in the spacious house that Ernst had built and fit their Plainview purchases of nice furniture into the rooms Carl had helped his father build. Carl kept farming the Schneider land.

The growing season brought Carl and Laura the news that their first child was coming. Alma Grace Schneider arrived on November 19, 1926. Laura named her for two dear friends from school.

Just a day or two after Grace was born, car thieves came to the farm pretending to need gas. A sleepy Carl told them that the side door to the garage was unlocked and that they could help themselves. They did help themselves – to his front tires and coils. They almost got the rear wheels off, too; Carl supposed that barking dogs might have scared them off.

Carl needed his car to go up to Crosbyton to help his sisters nurse their father. Ernst was still very ill from cancer. Edd Cox, a distant relative, let Carl use his car for a short trip to Crosbyton, and then Carl bought new wheels. After the purchase, a neighbor found his wheels in a straw stack six miles north, but the stolen coils were long gone.

1927 saw Ernst slowly losing his battle with cancer. But with the news of death came news of life. Carl and Laura were expecting another child.

Ernst died on August 29, 1927 and was buried in the cemetery at Cone.[39] Shortly afterward, Anna and Carl sold their interests in the Schneider farm to Emma, and eventually Fred sold his share to Minnie, who never married.[40]

But Carl and Laura built a two-room house on Laura's land. When they downsized from the large Schneider house to their own small one, they had to sell a great deal of the wedding furniture from Plainview at a loss.

Carl added features to the new house that showed he had been paying attention to Ernst's building decisions. Like Ernst, Carl had a well dug near his house. But Carl was done with hauling bucket after bucket of water up for stock. He installed a windmill to pump the water out, and he built trough and cool storage to keep what the wind pumped. He'd learned how to build with concrete by making troughs and tanks for Ernst.

Despite the loss of the better part of the housekeeping outfit, the new house was bright and cheerful, built by a carpenter named Mr. Jean with lumber brought in from Ralls. Soon after it was finished, Carl Glendon Schneider entered the world on March 6, 1928.

Gradually the house expanded; Carl paid for two more rooms to be built with lumber brought from Petersburg. And they needed the extra room when more children arrived. Clyde Kerlin Schneider was born on December 4, 1929, just a year and a half after his big brother. The two became inseparable quickly. A last brother, Finis Earl Schneider, arrived in 1931.

Two girls completed the family. Launa Joyce Schneider, named for Laura's mother, was born in 1934. JoAnn Virginia Schneider, who inherited Lizzie's middle name, Virginia, was born in 1937.

There was a midwife who came to help Laura with her births, someone named Granny Martin.[41] None of Laura's children were ever told much about her: who she was, what qualifications she had, or whether she were distantly related to them in some way. But whenever Laura delivered a child, there was Granny Martin.

Once when Granny Martin was visiting, the tribe of Schneider children were playing loudly and exuberantly outside. Laura kept getting up and calling to them to be careful, to watch what they were doing, and to make sure they didn't hurt themselves.

"Set down, and leave them be," Granny Martin admonished.

"But what if they get hurt playing like that?" Laura worried.

"One of them could break an arm."

"Well, honey," Granny Martin reasoned. "Sometimes they do that."

In the stories Laura's children tell, you may wonder how they escaped with so few injuries. Farms may not be safe, but they do give children wide spaces to play and much scope for the imagination. The stories that follow remember a time full of pranks and punishments, love and friendship, and the small ties that weave together into a strong bond.

It's a childhood the six Schneider siblings wouldn't trade for any other.

Chapter Five (5)
Alma Grace Schneider Winn

I had a very happy childhood.

We were very poor, and I'm sure that life was difficult for my parents, raising so many little children so near in age during the depression years. But mother was a good manager and a hard worker. She always had a garden, and she canned the produce. She also made me nice clothes, often from feed sacks. Even when times were hard, I was never hungry, and I always had clothes to wear.

Raising so many small children must have been hard on my mother. She was thirty when I was born and forty-two by the time JoAnn arrived. She must have been tired, but she was also patient.

I remember how pleased my mother was when my third grade teacher told her that my lunches were the nicest in the room. It seems to me that my sandwiches were often made from red beans. As I think about it now, I'm sure some of the things we had to eat were because there was nothing else. But my stomach was full, and it was fine.

We ate a lot of red beans and corn meal mush, in addition to the garden stuff. And Mother and Daddy kept chickens and cows and pigs; so we always had milk and butter and eggs and meat. I don't remember ever feeling deprived. I guess most people didn't have much more than we did.

I know Christmas was a difficult time for Mother, as she had so little money to spend on presents for us. But we always had something. I remember some nice doll furniture she made for me – a chair from a salt box, and a couch from a cocoa can. One year I got the book *Little Women*.

Daddy got us a horse named Jelly Bean, and we rode him for fun. My brothers made a little sled for Jelly Bean to pull; so sometimes we could ride on that. There was always something to do when we were finished with chores and schoolwork. And because Glen and Clyde were closest in age to me, we often played together.

They say that I came up with some mischievous ideas, but I think that they were more than capable of thinking up mischief on their own. We were not bad children, but we were very active. I often wonder how Mother survived rearing us!

Glen and Clyde got a bicycle, but they didn't want me to ride it. However, I rode it every time I could manage to get it. Then they would make me fall over. I still have scars on my arm from the time I rode into a barbed wire fence trying to get away from them.

We dug a hole in the ground for our own little cellar, which was much smaller than the cellar Mother used to store her canning, the one where we hid when there was a storm. I guess Daddy thought it might cave in on us; so he put a roof on it. The steps were so narrow that we thought Mother could not go down inside it and that it would be a good hiding place to avoid punishment.

But she was not to be outdone. When we ran down there, she just closed the door and sat on it until we begged to come out. Then she could discipline each one as he emerged!

Our house was very small, and we made a lot of noise when Mother wanted to talk on the telephone. So she made us go outside, which I didn't want to do. I can remember making lots of noise on the outside walls of the house. When we heard her say, "Just a minute, Iris," we knew we were about to be in trouble!

One piece of mischief Glen and Clyde and I caused was the shower bath. Using a brace and bit, we drilled holes in the barn roof over the cottonseed bin to make a shower. Two of us carried water, climbed on the roof, and poured the water through the holes on the other one inside. But Mother caught us before I got to have my turn; so I never got to use that shower!

We didn't consider that all of Daddy's cotton seed was right underneath our shower bath. When he found out how we'd wet all of that good seed, he was beside himself. I remember working late into the night, spreading the wet seed onto tarps to dry; Glen and Clyde and Daddy and I all had to help, though I generally only helped inside.

Mother had a poor memory, I thought. Once I did something for which she was going to punish me. I climbed on the barn and stayed for a long time. When I thought she would have forgotten the incident, I climbed down and went near where she was filling the kerosene lamps. She nabbed me; she had not forgotten!

I loved my grandfather, Granddad Kerlin. As I was the oldest grandchild, the only one older than I having died as a small

59

child, I spent a lot of time with him. As he lived only a mile from us, it was easy to walk to his house.

Before I could read, he would read the comics to me and insert my name. I remember combing his pretty white hair. And I would run around and around his chair while he tried to catch my legs with the crook of his cane. My delight was to spend the night with him and get to sleep with him in his feather bed.

So one of the best ways for Mother to discipline me was to ask what Granddad or Uncle Bert (Aunt Bernice's husband) would think of my actions. I wanted both of them to approve of me; so I always tried to live up to their expectations. For them to know of my small misdeeds would mortify me.

I remember one time Daddy whipped Glen, Clyde, and me. He was milking, and we stood on top of the barn roof and yelled to make the cow move. Every time we made the cow move, Daddy fell over. We thought we were safe because Daddy couldn't climb on top of the barn. But he did – and he brought a cornstalk with him to use on us!

Daddy usually didn't discipline us; Mother did. Though Mother was firm with us when we got into trouble, we always understood that she disciplined us in love. She was never upset with us long, and she never punished us without reason.

Our house was very small, and we had no indoor plumbing. We had an outdoor toilet. Once a week, we took baths in a large wash tub placed behind the coal stove when the weather was cold. During warm weather, we often put a tub of water outside to warm in the sun. That saved heating water on the kerosene cook stove.

I can remember very well when the REA (Rural Electrification Administration) came, and we had electricity. I was so pleased to be able to sit anywhere in the room to read rather than having to sit very near the kerosene lamp.

But having electricity did not mean that every aspect of life became modern overnight. For instance, we did not have a refrigerator until we moved to Plainview in 1943. And I can remember my mother doing the laundry by hand on a scrub board. I was probably eight or nine when she got a gasoline-powered washing machine. Until then, she did the laundry in a small building we called the well house because it was beside the water well.

Mother had so much work to do on the farm. I didn't realize at the time how much she did. When I grew older and asked her how she managed everything, she said, "Well, I didn't have PTA, WMU, or other outside activities. I just stayed home and worked my fool self to death."

I helped as much as I could, as all the children did. Mother always used to say, "Many hands make light work." She liked being outside in her garden, and I did not. So I'd help any way I could inside and leave the gardening to her. Thank goodness we didn't have to draw water by hand for all of that scrubbing and laundry and garden watering!

Our water was drawn by a wind-powered windmill. Because there was cool water flowing directly from underground, we had a water trough where we kept the milk and butter and other things that you'd keep in a refrigerator today. However, we could only have really chilled things like Jell-O in the winter, when the weather was so cold that we could put the dish in a cold room. We had no central heat.

Farmer school was only about a half mile from our house. There were three teachers and eight grades; so I was always in a room with more than one grade. The rooms were heated with big coal stoves. We had outside water faucets, but in winter we used a water bucket and dipper. The toilets were outdoors. We had no extra activities except a few sports like volleyball and baseball. And I was not good at any of them!

I remember going home from school many days to find Mother sitting at the sewing machine. I would stand beside her to do my homework. Friends said I was a good student because my mother did my schoolwork, but that wasn't true, though she did help me.

For one school assignment, she helped me write a poem that I still remember.

Bake, bake, bake,
How many cookies will it take
To feed three small boys
Bent on eating above all joys?

I was almost seven when I began first grade; so I was very mature and ready to learn. I never missed school, even when the weather was bad and Daddy had to walk and carry me or take me on a horse-drawn sled.

My first year the weather was so bad that often Gene Little-field and I were the only students. Because his parents operated the store next to the school, he was never absent. He was in the second grade. Seeing that we were the only pupils, I did most of the school work with him, and I completed both first and second grades in one year.

The weather during my childhood holds vivid memories. I was very afraid of electrical storms and thoughts of tornadoes.

Farmer was in what's called Tornado Alley. I often begged to go to the cellar – a hole dug in the ground with a roof on it. Being underground gave protection from tornadoes.

During those Depression years, the sand storms were very bad. I remember one when light from the sun was blotted out in the middle of the day. It became dark, and some people thought it was the end of the world.

I remember the special sand storm everyone always talks about. It was a Sunday, though I don't remember the exact date, and we were visiting our Priddy cousins. Granddad Kerlin was taking a Sunday afternoon nap at his house.

When the storm began to roll in, we children were playing outside, and we ran for shelter. At home, Granddad Kerlin woke up to find the windows dark. He thought he had slept straight through into the night!

The storms always scared me very badly. I can remember being very afraid I would die. But during a revival when I was about twelve years old (I don't remember whether it was a Methodist or Baptist revival), I asked Jesus into my heart. Since that time, I've not had that fear of dying.

But the storms were still a nuisance. Sand filled our cellar; it replaced water in our water tank and piled up to the top of our fences. Often we put wet cloths over our faces to filter out the sand. At night we dusted sand off the beds before going to sleep.

Of course, because of the wind and sand, there were no crops. With no cotton or grain to sell, farmers had no money. Some people lost everything in those years. We were very fortunate that Mother and Daddy owned their land. At least we still had a secure home, and we had what we raised to eat even when the crops failed.

Because we lived in the country during the Depression years and then World War II, there were not a lot of activities. Many people did not have money to buy cars, tires, or gasoline, and during the war, they were just not available. So people mostly just visited with each other.

I remember our family going in a wagon to visit friends, as we didn't have a car until I was well along in grade school. We had a monthly Community Night when various committees planned a program of some kind. I remember being on the program when I was about fourteen to tell about my trip to Louisiana and Alabama with Uncle Tom Kerlin, Granddad Kerlin's brother.

Mother used to tell a story about Uncle Tom. He was Granddad Kerlin's brother who lived in Louisiana. When Mother was a teenager, he was going to a conference in Chicago, and he offered to take Mother. They took the train up. Mother was peeling an apple with a favorite knife that had been a special gift. Trying to keep the seats clean, Uncle Tom threw the peelings out the window, along with Mother's favorite knife!

Of course, we did see the neighbors at church, which was a very important part of our lives. We met in the Farmer schoolhouse, as there was no separate church building. And the church at Farmer was a joint one with the Methodists and the Baptist; so the two denominations shared in our spiritual education.

One year we used Methodist Sunday school literature, and the next year we used Baptist literature. About once a month, a Methodist preacher from Ralls would come to conduct the service, and about once a month, a Baptist preacher would come. Daddy was a steward of the Methodist part, and Granddad was a deacon of the Baptist part. After we moved to Plainview,

Mother felt that the family should be united in church membership; so she joined the Methodist church.

We attended any special activities the church sponsored, but there weren't many. We never had VBS, choir, or missions organizations. One year, though, I was the Sunday school treasurer, a responsibility that required me to order the Sunday school literature. Granddad thought that would be good training for me.

Living with so many brothers and sisters was good training, too, though I didn't often appreciate it at the time. It seemed I never slept alone or went anywhere alone; a younger sibling was always with me. Back then, I got tired of it, but now I'm thankful for them all. I love them each so much.

Of course, Mother set a good example for me of sisterly love. Her sisters were all very dear to her, and Iris held a special place in her heart, as she'd been a sort of second mother to her. When Glen was a baby, Iris had to have surgery. Mother left Daddy in charge of Glen and me so that she could care for Iris while she recovered.

Aunt Iris lived with Granddad Kerlin until she got married. Then he went away and traveled for a little while before he came back and moved into her house, where she lived with Uncle Alvin. Granddad was ill for a short time, and then he died on May 18, 1941, when I was fourteen years old.

The spring he died was very wet. Because of Granddad's illness and that of a neighbor, Mr. Beavers, Daddy had not been able to work in the fields much. When he did get to plow, the weeds were higher than the tractor. And the rain made the dirt roads leading to Aunt Iris's house very muddy. We lived four miles from a paved road; when Granddad died, the hearse took four hours to travel those four miles.

I was the only grandchild who went to his funeral service, which was held in the Baptist church in Ralls. As I remember, it rained all during his service. He was buried in the Ralls cemetery. His wife, my grandmother Kerlin, died December 9, 1919, and was buried in the old Estacado cemetery.

Granddad homesteaded a section of land in the Farmer community, where he lived his whole adult life. He held many positions in the community – school trustee, Justice of the Peace, and deacon of the Baptist church. He helped move the first building to the site that would become Lubbock.

After Granddad died, the remaining 320 acres that had belonged to him was divided between his four daughters, giving each another 80 acres. Every daughter then had 160 acres of the original homestead. Our family moved into Granddad Kerlin's house and lived there for around two years before we sold our part of the property and moved to Plainview in 1943.

During that time, Glen, Clyde, and I rode the school bus to Ralls, about twelve miles, to attend high school. Because most of my high school years were during the Second World War, we had a basic curriculum and very few extra activities. I was seldom able to attend what little we did have, and I dated very little. I worked in the library and was an officer in my class. I do remember being in the school play my junior year.

Because of the teacher shortage, Mother began teaching at the Farmer school in 1943. She finished the school year before going to Plainview, where we had a small acreage with cows. Daddy did farm work there.

I graduated from high school in Ralls in May of 1943 with 37 students in my class. Several boys from my class had joined the military. All of my siblings graduated from Plainview High

School, which they attended after we moved.

Because of the war, there was not much farm help; so the summer after I graduated from high school, my brothers and I had plenty of jobs hoeing cotton. I think we made about fifty cents an hour. As we worked for different farmers, Glen and I often rode the motorcycle to work. I made enough money to buy some clothes and pay my college tuition for the first year.

Mother and I went to college at the same time. She had never finished the degree she began before she married; so when we moved to Plainview, she had a chance to resume her course-work. My first year in college, she was teaching during the day (she was JoAnn's first teacher) and going to school at night. She finished her degree in 1952, when she graduated from Wayland Baptist College. And in addition to the Farmer school, she taught in the Snyder community, Finny Switch, Seth Ward, and in the Plainview school system.

In the fall of 1943, after my summer of chopping cotton, I enrolled in West Texas State Teacher's College, which is now West Texas State University, part of the Texas A&M system. I was only sixteen. Life in Cousins dormitory was interesting and different for me.

The first semester I roomed with Lavern Exum, a childhood friend from home. After that, I had a number of roommates and made many good friends among them. My college years were a happy time for me.

I enjoyed working at the college library because I could get to know most of the students. After all, everyone had to come to the library. The library paid me fifty cents an hour, which gave me spending money and allowed me to buy my own clothes.

Though I had been raised both Methodist and Baptist, the

family united as Methodist after Mother joined the Methodist church in Plainview. But I leaned toward the Baptist denomination in college. I was active in the Baptist Student Union activities and First Baptist Church in Canyon, Texas, where I was baptized.

As teaching young children had long been my goal, I majored in Elementary Education. There were few male students enrolled in regular classes because most men my age were in military service. But we had servicemen training on our campus, which made life more interesting.

I had a summer job each summer. The summer of 1944, I worked in the tire rationing office in Plainview. Glen was working for an oil company. Most days he stopped for me to ride home for lunch on the back of his motorcycle or in the company truck.

I remember especially one day when he stopped, but thinking I was not going with him, he drove away. I saw him and ran after him. Every time I almost caught up, he sped away. I ran most of the way home, and by the time I got there, I was so hot and angry that I couldn't eat. I had Daddy drive me back to work immediately!

Glen will tell you that he never saw me, but I don't know about that. Glen has always had a strong sense of humor.

One summer I worked in sales at Montgomery Ward's. Another summer I worked at the Dimmit Co-op elevator, and then for several summers I worked at the Plainview Co-op Elevator.

After graduating from college in May 1947, I taught third grade in Perryton, Texas for two years. I made a good salary: $2,007 for the year! And as there were a number of single teachers, both male and female, we were able to have a pretty good social life.

In September of 1949, I moved to Albuquerque, New Mexico, where I taught third grade at 5 Points School. It was a good four years. There were many servicemen in Albuquerque; so there was a lot to do. I was active in First Baptist Church there.

At that church, I met Bill Winn at a church training group for singles. He was stationed at Sandia Base. Our first date, October 31, 1952, was dinner at the airport restaurant and a movie.

At dinner when I started to cut my head lettuce salad (a large wedge of lettuce with dressing), it fell off the plate onto the floor. I was so embarrassed that I said, "Oh well, I never liked lettuce anyway!" For years, Bill thought I didn't like lettuce!

Our first dates were mostly attending the Billy Graham tent revival. Afterwards, we had an A&W root beer. I have always told Bill that he married me because I was a cheap date!

We dated the four months until his discharge from the military, when he took a job in Frederick, Maryland with Ralph M. Parsons Company. I didn't see him again, nor meet his parents, until he and they came for our wedding! (It worked out well for me, but I don't recommend that plan!)

I finished my school year in Albuquerque, and we were married June 20, 1953 in the First Baptist Church of Plainview, Texas. Afterward, we flew to Washington, D.C., where Bill had left his car parked. It was my first long flight and the first time I was served a meal on a plane. I think it took about eight hours in a prop plane to fly from Lubbock to Washington. We spent a week in Virginia – Williamsburg, Jamestown, etc. – for our honeymoon before we settled down in Maryland.

It's hard to say when you leave home for good. Moving during my senior year in high school to Plainview meant leaving the home where I'd been raised. I went to college at sixteen, but I still lived at home in Plainview during the school breaks. And Mother and Daddy were always there when I needed them.

I got my first official, full-time, adult job when I was twenty. I lived nearly two hundred miles north of where I'd grown up; so I wasn't home nearly as often. But I still came home for holidays; there was nowhere else I belonged as much as I belonged with Mother and Daddy and my brothers and sisters.

I moved out of state at twenty-two, which was another degree of separation. And then I married at twenty-six. The start of my new family was definitely a parting from my first family. The last time we were all together, before we all married and scattered, was the Christmas of 1952. That was Mother's favorite Christmas, and it's a dear one for me, too.

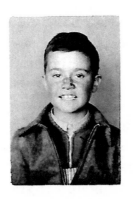

Chapter Six (6)
Carl Glendon Schneider

I was born in March of 1928, just about fifteen months after Grace and eighteen months before Clyde. The fact that the president of the United States when I was born was Calvin Coolidge really dates me!

My parents named me, their first boy, Carl after my father. I have no idea where Mother got my middle name, Glendon, but I've never liked it. I don't use it at all now. The minute I got into the service and couldn't be confused in daily life with my father, I changed it.

When I was a toddler, Mother had to interrupt giving me a bath because a political candidate came to the kitchen door. Mother shut me in the pantry so that I wouldn't drown in the bath, and she spoke for a few minutes to the politician before she could politely show him the door.

When she came to get me, I was covered head to toe in syrup. That was me from the beginning: always ready for a little bit of fun and mischief, and more than a little bit impatient.

I've also been adventurous and curious all my life. Not many years after the syrup incident, rural electricity came to our part of Texas, and workers dug holes near our property to hold the electrical poles. I just had to investigate one, and I got stuck. Mother came and pulled me out.

Mother was a constant in my life when I was young. She was a really hard worker who always kept us in line. Mother's truck garden had rows of beans and tomatoes and all kinds of vegetables. We had the windmill for irrigation; so she could run an irrigation ditch down each row. She'd raise a lot of vegetables, and then all the women would get together for canning, using big glass jars and storing for the winter.

Daddy would butcher a pig and a calf. He rented a freezer in town to save the dressed meat. Besides, we always had plenty of chickens for eggs and meat. We had milk and butter from our cows. So we always had plenty to eat. We didn't ever go hungry, though we didn't have much money.

I don't know how Mother did it. She didn't have but half a dozen pots and pans and a coal oil stove where you'd put the kerosene in at the end of the stove, but she always had good meals. It always tasted good to all of us kids. I just don't know how she did that.

My favorite memory of home is when we were all around the big, round table. Everybody would be laughing and carrying on, acting silly, telling jokes, and kidding each other during meals. I remember Mother laughing. She had a great sense of humor. Daddy wasn't a big joker, but he grinned all the time. I think he liked hearing the rest of us.

Mother also stayed busy washing and sewing for us so that we had clean clothes. She would lengthen our pants hems so that they fit us as long as the fabric lasted. She also made all of the dresses for the girls out of color-printed flour sacks. The only things we ever bought were sugar and flour and a couple of other things we couldn't raise on the farm. Mother was very frugal.

And her books – she was an incessant reader. She'd always have a book propped up wherever she was working. If she was working in the kitchen, she'd have a book along in there with her. She read just all kinds of books.

We didn't have a library close, not like you have now. So she must have borrowed them from neighbors and friends, and maybe she got some from the library at Ralls. I don't know her actual favorites.

But she was a wonderful lady. She was very motivational, and I never heard her say a bad word about anybody. No matter how tough the times got, she'd say, "Well, the good Lord is going to take care of us." She had a really strong faith; so that got us off to a good start.

She loved poetry, and she loved flowers. She'd read all kinds of poetry to us. Robert Frost was her favorite. I've got several books now that have been my favorite all those years. She always liked flowers and had flowers in the house as well as planted around it; that's about all we had to color up the place.

Like most women at the time, she wore dresses every day. She probably had two dresses and an apron. All the women wore aprons then when they cooked so that the food wouldn't ruin their dresses.

Mother was the belle of the ball before she got married, just Miss Personality. She organized most of the social activities in town. Her father, Granddad Kerlin, was the patriarch of the whole area there. They all called him Uncle John. His name was John Peter, and I've always wondered whether he was named after the two disciples, John and Peter.

Granddad was gray haired; I thought he was God until I was about five or six years old. He was a very stern kind of man. I think he had a good sense of humor under that stern countenance.

He was Mother's hero. She had great respect for her dad. And I think that's why all of us respected our parents so much, because we were watching her. That sort of thing follows on through generations.

As far as Mother's mother, she didn't really talk a lot about her. Granddad Kerlin homesteaded out in Farmer, and he must have been in his thirties when the Thorntons moved onto the adjacent land. Grandmother was only sixteen years old when they courted. He married her when she was seventeen or eighteen. She died fairly young.

Granddad was big on education. Mother went to two years of college and studied education, and then her mother died. I know she would have liked to have finished, but she had to come home and help take care of her sisters.

Mother and Dad got married just before the Depression hit. They built this small little house, about eight hundred square feet, and that's where most of us were raised.

Mother was determined for each of us to get a college education. She hammered on that almost from the time we could walk. She valued education so highly that when we were older and she had time away from farm work, she taught school and then went back to college herself. She finally finished her undergraduate degree after age fifty! Mother was a super lady.

However, when we were young and Daddy was farming, she didn't have time to do much else other than work, except for organizing the all-day preaching and dinner on the grounds that we'd have occasionally.

All the women would bring this wonderful food, and we kids would just pig out on it all. We'd always have plenty of food – I enjoyed that. When we were growing up, you could eat a lot of that good food, and it wouldn't hurt you. There were all kinds of fresh vegetables, and ham and chicken and beef. And some folks had fruit trees. Granddad Kerlin had trees with fruit.

The preacher the town had invited would start out in the morning, and we'd have preaching for about an hour. Then we'd go eat. And then he'd go back and preach again.

We all loved the food. We'd get together and play baseball there. Mother would organize many of those all-day events.

We had a lot of activities at the church and at the school house. I remember a lot of fun things we did. The teachers would come up with different plays, and we had itinerant preachers come through. We didn't have a regular preacher; we had all kinds of different preachers. We'd have them stay with us.

Mother was just a wonderful lady, but she was not a neat housekeeper. She was a clean housekeeper, but things just stacked up all over the house. I fussed at her one day, and she said, "They're not coming to see the house. They're coming to see us."

Though we always had company, I could never figure where people slept! It was amazing how Mother managed.

Clyde and I had a double bed in one bedroom, and Finis had his single bed. We had a little closet; of course, we didn't have many clothes anyway, just a couple of hangers with some shirts and overalls. Mother and Dad had a bedroom. The girls had to pull a bed out of the couch, the sofa, and the three of them slept together. We had a pot-bellied stove in the middle of the living room, and that was it. It was pretty snug living.

Like Mother, Daddy was a hard worker, too, although his work must have been frustrating because of the Dust Bowl. When I was grown and gone I was talking with him one day, I asked him, "How much cash did you average every year during those Depression years?" I knew that some years, we didn't make a crop.

He told me, "I averaged about $250 a year." And that two-fifty might be a couple of thousand dollars now, but it definitely wasn't much. Despite that scarcity, we always had enough for shoes, for school, and for church.

Everybody thinks of the Dust Bowl being like *The Grapes of Wrath*, that it's dull and grey and everybody's worried. The whole decade wasn't a dull, gray, unhappy time. You get that impression from the black and white photos, but they're not the whole story.

The Dust Bowl was hard on our parents; I'm not saying it wasn't hard having no money and enduring the hardships they went through. I know that the parents had a lot more concerns. However, my parents, even though they did shoulder a lot of responsibility, participated in social activities and provided a lot of good food.

As kids, we didn't realize all the financial hardships that our parents went through. I'm actually grateful for the place and time and way I was raised - I wouldn't swap it for anything. It was wonderful. We had a great time. You have to understand that from a kid's standpoint, we had fun. My dad just didn't have much cash.

I think it was different for us out on the farm than it was in the cities, where folks really did have a tougher time. They didn't have food, and they were out of work. What made a big difference for us, too, was that we owned the land. A lot of folks around us went broke paying for a mortgage on the land and paying for feed for animals and seed. But Mother had a fourth of Granddaddy Kerlin's land; so we were okay.

What I remember most about the Dust Bowl, besides the good times with my family, is those storms rolling in. A dust storm was a rolling row of dust with a hot wind behind it, and it would be just like a roll on the ocean, but forty thousand feet high. Most of the time, there was no thunder or lightning, just wind. I don't even remember a lot of sound to it. I just remember the sight of it rolling in.

You couldn't even see across the room sometimes while it was storming, but of course, we had no insulation to the house. So dust would pile up on the windowsills, and you'd have to turn your plate upside down if you were going to eat, because that sand blowing in all the time covered everything. You'd have to shake your sheets out at night, too. Otherwise, you'd feel gritty, because the sheets had sand all in them.

And tumbleweeds would roll against the fences, and then the sand would pile up there so that the cows could walk right over them. And in the winters (we had some really bad winters) the snow would cover over the tumbleweeds and the sand. I spent half my time chasing cows and pigs all over the county, trying to catch them.

Those storms were dangerous, just like a snowstorm. If you saw one coming, you'd get home, because you sure didn't want to be out in one. We also had a lot of thunderstorms and a lot of tornadoes. We had a cellar, and Daddy would get out and watch the sky. When he saw what looked like a tornado coming, or a really bad thunderstorm, we'd all head down to the cellar, which was very cozy. (By cozy, I mean tight quarters!)

We had an old lantern down there, and Mother would read us poetry while we waited for skies to clear. She'd read poetry to keep us occupied, and Daddy would go up and look around. And when he'd finally decide that the rain had gone by or the storm had passed, we could get out. We did that a lot.

The land looked afterward like a sea of dust. The sand would have piled up against all the fences and against the house.

Daddy didn't get a crop for seven of the years during the Dust Bowl, but it wasn't all due to the storm. It was the drought. We just didn't get rain. If we did get a rain shower, it came at the wrong time. We didn't have any irrigation except for the windmill, and we used that water for the house and the garden and the animals.

If we did get a crop, then a hail storm would come through and hail it out at the last minute. I don't know how my dad kept his sanity during those years. I look back now, and I can appreciate all that he went through. It was really tough.

There are parts of documentaries that talk about the driving dust blinding some of the animals outside. We had barns, plenty of space in the barns for the animals to go inside when it was really coming in from the north. I don't remember any of our animals going blind or being damaged like that because of the dust.

And even with the tremendous pressure my parents faced, I never heard them arguing in front of us at all. Ever. They might have fussed behind the scenes when we were gone to school or something, but they always seemed to get along. That was a great experience for us.

We didn't make a big deal out of birthdays. I'm sure that Mother had a cake and candles for us, and then she'd fix whatever anybody wanted to eat. I don't recall a lot of holidays. We worked six days a week and went to church, and then we went to school.

And then about Christmas – you'd get one gift, and maybe an orange. I never saw a banana until I went into the Air Force. You just didn't see bananas then. That's why I have a banana every morning now.

I got a BB gun for Christmas one year. That was my favorite present. Of course, we could always use Daddy's .22 rifle. Uncle Bert was a deputy sheriff. He'd keep a gunny sack of .22 bullets in the back of his car. Whenever he'd visit, we'd get a big double handful of bullets from him so that we could shoot tin cans and hunt rabbits.

Mother should have been Saint Teresa. She raised six kids to be responsible and educated and love each other. That was quite an achievement, considering how different we all were.

Grace was always the teacher and sort of the honcho; she taught us all to read before we went to school. She was always the ringleader, and sometimes she'd get us into trouble. Mother would blame us boys, while she'd get away and take the fifth.

But anyway, she was a good sister, really loving to all of us kids. She's been that way all of her life,the mother hen of the family.

Clyde was sort of messy, and late. Daddy used to say that he'd sit down and wait so that he could be late, if we were getting ready to go to church or work. Daddy would always have to fuss at him. The rest of us would be ready to go, and he wouldn't be ready to move. When he joined the Air Force, he learned to be on time!

He and I were the best of buddies. We were like twins from the time we grew up. We did everything together. He was a really good brother.

Finis was in the background, and I carry a little bit of guilt about that, because we tended to ignore him. He was the pesky little brother that was always trailing us around. Finis was very quiet, while Clyde and I were the ones coming up with new ideas and so forth.

Because Finis was always in the shadows, I really can't remember him getting involved in any of the things that Clyde and I got into. He was just always off on the side somewhere.

I asked him one time when we had a family reunion, "Did that really bother you?" And he said, "No, it didn't." He just did his own thing. But he was a good young kid who turned out with a good personality as a really good man.

Joyce was the Erma Bombeck of the family, just as funny as can be – she always had something funny to say. One thing I remember about her: she always thought that her birthday was "the next day of May." One time she said, "I'm going to smoke cigarettes when I grow up, even if I have to get behind the door to do it!" Of course, she didn't do it. But she was a cute little girl and a lot of fun.

And JoAnn was always the perky one, sort of the spoiled one of the family. She was the baby and a real cute little gal.

Clyde and I used to hold a nickel out or a dime and see if Joyce or JoAnn would get our shoes or something and come back in ten or fifteen seconds. Of course, they'd always be late and wouldn't earn the dime. So years later I gave each one of them twenty dollars when we were having a family reunion. I said, "I hope that will make up for the fact that I shorted you on all those dimes!"

All of us kids were very fortunate to have had a Mother like ours. Mother made you feel like you were the most important kid out of all of the six. I never felt any jealousy, and I never felt like she favored any one of us. It was a really unique way to manage all six of us.

She was always really positive, and she'd tell us, "You do whatever you want to do, so long as it's honest." And she'd say, "Your dad wants you to stay here and farm, and I know you don't want to do it. So you boys get out, and you girls, and you do whatever you want to do." So that's why we all left when we grew up. She gave us that freedom and encouragement.

Though she rarely traveled in her life, she had a really adventurous spirit. She would have really liked to have the money to have a nice house and travel. I told her one time that she should have been a banker's wife. And she said, "No, I wanted to raise you kids on the farm. And it worked out great. You kids are my legacy."

She was very proud of her children. She put every bit of her effort into us. In many ways I'm like her, because I'm chicken-hearted – tenderhearted, you would say. I'm not a hard-nosed kind of guy. At the same time, I'm like my father because I'm a hard worker. He was dedicated to do his job and do it right.

Dad was a good, solid member of the community. He had all of his farming friends, and when they'd get together, they'd talk about the crops. Those were just neighbors; he didn't have one good buddy like some guys do. But he was well-respected, and I think a lot of the farmers would come by and talk to him about planting and get his ideas.

Every day Daddy would get up early. In the winter, he would fix the fires before we got up. In the summer, he went straight out to the barn. And then he'd just work solid all day long.

He'd go milk the cows, feed the pigs and the chickens, muck out the barn, and then head to the fields. There he would plow, plant, hoe, harvest - whatever we had to do according to the growing season. He would work all day long. Then many times he'd go shuck corn in the barn after supper. He just worked solid; he was a really good worker.

I'm sure that working with Daddy all those years made me into a workaholic. If I was plowing a row with the tractor that wasn't exactly straight, Dad would tell me to go back and redo it. I would. He was a real stickler for doing things right; so I learned to be that way in the service and in business.

Dad didn't tell me much about his parents, but I got the feeling that my mother was like his, just a sweet, wonderful woman. But she died when he was very young; so he didn't get a lot of parental guidance from her.

His dad was from Germany; he didn't speak very good English. And he wouldn't let my dad or the rest of his children learn to speak German. He said, "You're American. You speak English." So Daddy never did learn German. I think that was a mistake. I think Grandfather Schneider should have had his kids learn German.

Apparently, he was just scratching for a living out there on his dry land farm in West Texas. He was not really the outdoorsman that Granddad Kerlin was; I think because of the language. I don't really remember any stories about him other than him working hard and doing his job.

Daddy worked so long with his dad that he got used to doing things the way his dad had done them. We plowed with horses until I was about ten or twelve. We'd go to town on a Saturday, and many times before we got a car (I think I was about ten or twelve before we got a car), he and I would go in a wagon with a couple of horses and he'd buy flour or sugar or whatever we needed. And that's when he'd do his visiting with all of the neighbors down the main street.

And until we got a car, I don't know that Mother went to town a lot. Daddy was used to men doing everything outside the home, and Mother always seemed to stay home and hold down the fort. He'd go to town and come back. And I always wondered if behind closed doors there was a little bit of tension because she would have liked to go to town sometimes more. But as I said, we never saw any tension between them.

Dad wasn't really big on doing things in a new way. Clyde and I were always coming up with new ideas on how to do things cheaper, better, and faster. And he'd say, "Why don't you just do it the way I've always been doing it?"

It just irritated him, because we were always saying, "Well, why don't we plow this field this way? Why don't we do this thing this way?" And he'd say, "Why don't you boys do it the way it's supposed to be done?" We had a lot of imagination and were constantly looking for new things to get into.

He really didn't relax a lot in the evenings. He'd always take a nap for about fifteen, twenty minutes after the noon meal, which we called dinner in those days. We had breakfast, dinner, and supper.

I remember how Dad liked to eat syrup on his sausage. I still do that; it was just one of those things. And he liked to eat pinto beans. So do I. I'll go down to Henpeck Village Market in Franklin, TN and have a bowl of pinto beans about every couple of weeks. That brings back memories.

After dinner, he'd just stretch out on the floor and nap for fifteen and twenty minutes, because I know he got up before we did. And then he'd be working after we went to bed.

He never had any real hobbies, never had time to do anything. He never went on vacation; he couldn't get away from the cows. You had to milk the cows every morning and night, and nobody else could come in and milk. We never took a vacation with my mother and dad while I was growing up.

I did everything that Daddy told me, just like the rest of the kids. I went out and milked cows and fed pigs and curried horses and chopped cotton. He gave orders, and you didn't argue about them. He'd say, "Go milk the cows," and it was just, "Yes, sir." You'd go out and milk the cows. There was no arguing or backtalk either to Mother or to Dad; you just did what they told you.

I never did particularly enjoy farm work. Once when I was small, I saw an airplane swooping and climbing and doing acrobatics over our cotton field. It was amazing to me, and from that day on, I wanted to fly one. I knew I wasn't meant to be a farmer, though I never shirked my chores.

The boys helped outside, and the girls helped inside. I don't think the girls did anything outside. They may have made an attempt at some things, but they didn't tend to the animals or work the fields. And we boys didn't do anything on the inside.

So you know, I can't boil water. I didn't learn to cook or do any of the domestic things.

That was the way it was. The girls were all helping Mother. They'd go out in the garden, gather peas, help her with the canning, set the table, and help Mother do all the chores around the house.

Looking back, I love the fact that we worked close to our parents. We were there with them all day long. It's such a contrast to families now. You'd watch them do all that they did. My Daddy's favorite term was, "Make yourself useful." With him around, you didn't sit around on your butt all the time. And Mother's favorite saying was, "Many hands make light work."

Daddy was very moral. He never gambled, never drank, and never swore. The closest he ever came when something went really wrong, if a cow ran away or something, was to say, "Darn, darn, darn!" He really didn't like swearing.

Dad was super honest. He'd never cheat anybody out of a nickel. And Mother was the same way. One time Clyde and I found eggs and tried to sell them to Uncle Alvin, the storekeeper. Mother made us take the candy and money we'd gotten right back there.

Uncle Alvin wasn't my uncle initially. He came to Farmer and opened up that country store and met Aunt Iris. She had been living with Granddad Kerlin and taking care of him. She was one of the only eligible old maids around, and he was one of the only bachelors. So they sort of teamed up and ended up getting married.

After they got married, he was always nice. He'd give you a penny gumdrop.

I enjoyed Farmer, where we were sort of the elite of the community, I always figured. Mother would always tell us, "You kids come from good stock." And of course, both grandfathers had homesteaded there. We weren't stuck up at all, but it always felt like we were the leaders of the community.

Clyde and I were the leaders of all the boys, and we were always coming up with stuff to do. They'd follow us on their bicycles toward whatever mischief we were going to get into. And at home, of course, we played with our brother and sisters and the neighbors.

One of the games we used to play was Annie Over. We'd have one group of kids on one side of the house and another on the other side. Then we'd throw the ball over the house. Whoever caught the ball would run around the house and try to tag a kid on the other side.

We would play softball, too. We had a ball of binder twine for the softball, and our bat was a two-by-four that Daddy had whittled down into shape. We had a couple of old feed sacks filled with dirt for our bases. We would all get out and play ball about every second we didn't have to spend doing chores. I still like to play softball.

We had the Nobles living next to us, and they had six kids, too. So they'd come over, and with the twelve of us we could have a real game.

We played a lot of dominoes, but Daddy didn't like cards. He probably associated them with gambling; he was very firm on that stand. But Grace loves to play cards now; she and Bill are big card players, maybe because she couldn't play while growing up.

We played with our cousins when we saw them. John Robert was Aunt Mae and Uncle Jim's son, and he was a city boy. One of our sheds had an eave so low that the horse could just barely duck his head and go underneath. We would put John Robert on that horse, and it would scrape him off every time right into the horse manure. We thought that was really funny.

For school, I attended a three-room schoolhouse. I don't think that I had any favorite lessons. I just wanted to get out and fly airplanes. School was a drag for me. Instead of having kids lined up in a bunch of desks, they need a much more creative atmosphere. I didn't use one fifth of one percent of my brain-power going through school, because it was all a piece of cake.

I wanted to get involved in a lot of other different things. I wanted to fly airplanes and travel. Sitting through school was not interesting to me. I never had homework, because I could finish lessons quickly. After that, I'd be looking out the window at the clouds and the birds flying past. I wanted to get out and get going!

I had seven years of school after first grade, then two in Ralls and two in Plainview. Part of the reason I could go through lessons so fast was the fact that during my seven years in Farmer, I was in a school house that used the same books every year. After first grade, I'd heard every lesson I was going to hear all the way through from the other kids.

My two favorite classmates in the Farmer school would have been my girlfriends, Doris and Lucille. I didn't have any favorite school mates among the boys. Clyde and I did everything together; whatever one did, the other joined in.

I always had this idea that you ought to be able to do what you wanted to do in school, what really turned you on. Luckily for me, I did have some teachers who knew I wanted to fly and explore, and they directed my reading to books in my line of interest.

That's one thing that's great about a small environment. The teachers can pay attention to individual students. Now with the kids in one big room and with all of the discipline problems, they can't give the individual attention that we all need.

Also, we're geared to the left brain in the schools. We really train that left brain with facts, but we don't engage the right brain: creativity, ingenuity, and imagination. We need to do more of that right brain development.

In my school, I never did care much for the superintendent, Mr. Legg. I was never bad, but I was on the edge of things. And I did get into some mischief. I never have cared for anyone talking down to me, and he did that. As a kid, you just don't forgive those things.

One time we were playing baseball in a field that had an irrigation ditch running around it. We had one ball, and it fell in. He came out there and just chewed me out for getting the ball wet. I was playing catcher, and I missed. You don't forget being chewed out in public like that.

Mr. Legg ended up coloring my management style. When I grew up and was in charge of other people, I was firm, friendly, and fair. I never chewed anybody out. If I didn't like something somebody did, I'd invite them inside and close the door and talk about it. I never got all upset in meetings and threw pencils like some people did. I wanted to be the opposite of what I saw other leaders and managers doing.

My favorite teacher was Ima Smith, who ended up marrying a man who became governor of Texas. Jimmy Dean, who became famous in country music, was a classmate of mine. When he opened his sausage factory in Plainview, he hosted a reception at the country club and invited the governor and his wife.

I went to that reception. During the event, there was a receiving line for the governor and his wife. I was standing in line, and she spotted me. Before I could open my mouth, she said, "Now don't say anything – you're Glen!" She remembered me, and she hadn't seen me since about first grade. She was a wonderful lady, and I was in love with her when I was small.

Church was a regular part of our lives growing up. Mother read the Bible to us, and we went to Sunday school and church every Sunday. You knew that unless you died, you were going to be there.

Mrs. Reed was my Sunday school teacher back in Farmer. And I was kind of wild and crazy – Clyde and I had a motorcycle. We bought an old motorcycle, and we tore it down to the last nut and bolt. Then we put it back together again, and it ran great.

One day I was riding by Mrs. Reed's house. She lived up on a hill, and she came running down to the road, flapping her apron. I skidded to a stop in front of her fence. She shook her finger at me and said, "Son, you're going to get killed in the next month if you keep on riding that motorcycle!" She turned around and went back to her house.

So when I started flying jet fighters, I'd fly low over her house and do slow rolls. But she was a dear soul and a good person.

The biggest part of my religious education was the influence of my parents. Mother and Dad both had a strong faith. If they hadn't had that, they would never have made it through the Depression. We always prayed before meals. Mother read the Bible to us, and she read poetry.

That built faith in me. I always knew that the Lord was guiding me, wherever I was. I've been close to death many, many times flying jet fighters in two wars. And when I land alive, I think, "Well, Lord, I guess you have more work for me to do." When I'd get up in the morning, I'd say, "I've got two bosses: the good Lord and my wife. And I'd better listen to both of them!"

I believe in Jesus Christ, and I believe I'm going to him right away when I kick out of this planet. It keeps me going; I've just never had any real doubt about that.

Now, when I was a small boy, I didn't like the church building. It had no air conditioning. And some of these preachers would just go on and on and on and on. We'd be kept two hours and more in there. And as a kid, you're squirming, and it's hot.

I remember one preacher who had a Ph.D. – he talked way above my head. I couldn't understand the really theoretical stuff. But I stayed in all of the chaplain programs in the Air Force. Since I've retired, I've always been in some kind of a Bible study and attended church services. I'd say that religion is fundamental to my beliefs.

In 1943, when I was fifteen, Dad sold the farm, and we moved to town. And I know he would have liked to stay there and have us boys run the farm, but we didn't like the hard farm life.

Mother wanted us to move to Plainview and get a broader view of life. She knew that we weren't seeing much while we were stuck on the farm. And also, she knew we boys didn't want to stay there. The only things I liked about farming were riding a tractor, a motorcycle, or a horse. I wasn't big on the other things.

Uncle Jim was the only guy that Daddy never liked. He was a ne'er do well, and he married Aunt Mae. He and Daddy never got along because Jim was harum-scarum, never successful at anything. The cousin we used to scrape off Jelly Bean into the horse manure, John Robert, was his son.

Dad offered to sell Mother's share of the Kerlin land to Uncle Jim, and Uncle Jim promised to pay $35 per acre. That's probably several hundred dollars an acre now. When they got ready to sign, Jim said, "No, I'm only going to pay you $30 an acre." We'd already made the commitment to move up to Plainview and had to sell. Daddy was really upset about that.

Jim bought our land, and Aunt Mae already had her quarter. He bought Aunt Bernice's, too. So Jim had three-quarters of the original section.

Aunt Iris kept hers. Her two children, Forest and Martha, hired a farmer who farmed it for them on a third and fourth basis. That meant that the renting farmer took over the farm, managed it, and took 2/3 of the grain and ¾ of the crop. If you owned the land, you got a third and a fourth as your rent payment.

We were missed in the Farmer community. A dear woman in our church wrote a poem about our moving away that meant a lot to our whole family.

CARL AND LAURA SCHNEIDER'S FAMILY MOVE AWAY[42]

They are leaving us now, our friends of the years,
So bright with sunshine, and sprinkled with tears;
They are moving away, and well do we know
How it grieves our hearts, to see them go;
So long have we known them, they seem a part
Of the Farmer Community's very heart;

Here they grew up and loved and were wed,

Carl Glendon Schneider

And here have they lived, near the old homestead;
Here their children were born, sweet Alma Grace,
Slender of form and fair of face;
Carl Glendon, one of Farmer's own boys,
Sharing in all of their school day joys;

Clyde Kerlin was also a comrade true,
No matter if [skies] be gray or blue;
And Finis Earl, the younger lad,
Sturdy and manly, serene and glad;
And a fair little girl, Launa Joyce,
With smiling face and happy voice;

And sweet [JoAnn], the youngest one,
Mother's small helper and full of fun;
We shall miss them all, each cherished face,
They will leave in our hearts an empty place;
And may the new home, to which they go,

Bring them the best, that their lives can know;
May it hold it's fill of the purest joys,
That life can bring to girls and boys;
May it bring to our friends, that we hold so dear,
More peace, with every passing year;

And more of love than our tongue can tell,
May God bless the Home they have builded so well!

WRITTEN FOR FARMER COMMUNITY,
IN SINCERE FRIENDSHIP –
FLORA SMITH DEAN

We were the lodestar for that community, and when we moved from Farmer to Plainview, that center of gravity was gone. Like Mrs. Dean said, the Farmer community just went down from there, because Mother was sort of the anchor in the community, organizing many activities.

Around the same time we moved, a lot of other farmers started moving into Ralls and farming from there. Then other, bigger farmers came in to plant and harvest. Most of the other farmers moved into town and managed their land for third and fourth shares after we moved away.

I'd call those other folks windshield farmers, because they'd hire someone else who was getting out and doing all the work, and they'd drive down in a pickup truck and see how things were going through the windshield.

There were a lot of guys in town who'd never farmed. They'd hire somebody who wanted to stay there and farm. That managing farmer would have big farm equipment, enough to allow them to take over several hundred acres. The little family farms dwindled after we moved away. Very few of them had animals. The small farmers put them in stock pens and consolidated everything in Lubbock and Ralls and in certain other places.

I think that many of the World War II veterans felt like we did, that they didn't want to come back on the farm. Most of them went on to college and got town jobs. That accelerated the change in the culture in that part of the country. That happened all through the Midwest – through Colorado, Texas, New Mexico, and Kansas.

When we moved to Plainview, my parents bought a small dairy. We still had cows to milk, but we had a milking machine so that we wouldn't have to milk by hand. Clyde and I lived in the milk house until Mother and the girls and Finis arrived and we got the main house ready. Daddy went back and forth between Farmer and Plainview until school was out that spring and Mother and the smaller children could move.

We had ten acres in Plainview, large enough that you could have a house and a barn and tend any kind of animal on them. And you could raise some crops and have a pretty large truck garden for vegetables. Daddy had some row crops there at the dairy on the edge of town. It was a working dairy; so our chores changed from field work to dairy work.

I tried to talk him into subdividing the ten acres and putting some houses up on a smaller lot to sell, because I knew that a lot of the men coming home from World War II were going to need houses. Later, Daddy ended up selling the land to someone else, and that's exactly what the buyer did. He put up some houses, and he made some really good money.

Our family was a lot like the rest of the families in Plainview at that time. Not many people had very much money. And there were quite a few small farms like ours at the edge of town.

In Plainview, Grace, Clyde, Finis, and I got jobs. Grace chopped cotton in the summer and then went to college. Clyde worked in a garage part time. Finis did several different odd jobs.

Most of the older guys were off at World War II, leaving vacancies back home. So I got a job when I was sixteen driving an oil truck for Magnolia Petroleum Company. I drove out to the farms and filled up the gas tanks for tractors and irrigation wells and filling stations. That was a big responsibility for a teenager.

I also worked for some farmers, doing some plowing. During the summers, both Clyde and Finis went north to the wheat harvest. A guy in Lubbock would take them north all the way to the Canadian border working the harvest for wheat before they started back to school. I never did that. I did help a farmer north of Amarillo with his plowing for one summer.

Aunt Minnie was our old maid aunt; she never married. She always held that against Daddy. She said she'd had a beau once, and he'd chased him off. She sure was a pretty lady, and she loved all of us kids.

Aunt Minnie had kept the Ernst Schneider land. She bought shares when Dad moved to the Kerlin land and Fred moved to California. She had a man to farm it up until right before she died. She lived off that land; she got a third of the grain and a fourth of the crop every year. But she didn't always live there; she moved first to Plainview and then on to Lubbock.

One summer I was plowing around Amarillo for a man who wasn't very nice. Aunt Minnie invited me to come with her to Arizona and work as a cowboy on Uncle Orville's ranch. So I quit the Amarillo job and went to Arizona.

The farmer in Amarillo wasn't too happy with me, because he had a hard time finding anyone to replace me by that time in the season. But that summer was a great experience, and it began my love affair with Arizona, where I later lived for forty years. I loved ranch work, being up in the mountains and riding horses every day.

When I got to high school, I had a good friend named Tom Babb. He spent a lot of time with both Clyde and me. For friends, I think I gravitated to the other boys who had come in from the country and were living on small farms like ours.

In our free time in Plainview, Clyde and I spent time with our friends from school. We had a lot of fun together. We had our motorcycle to ride, and we got a car.

We bought an old Model A. One time we were going to Amarillo, and the radiator sprung a leak. They didn't pressurize the radiators in those old cars. So being very ingenious, we went to a store and got a five-cent piece of bubble gum. Then we chewed bubblegum to put on the leak. That stopped it! We were always pretty innovative.

Five cents for bubble gum – prices sure have gone up. I remember that if I was going out to Lubbock or somewhere, Mother would give me fifteen cents. I could get a hamburger and a Coke for fifteen cents.

I graduated from high school in 1945. Then I went to one year of college at Texas Tech because I got a scholarship of thirty dollars a month for room and board.

I was what they called a Lone Star farmer. Sears and Roebuck held a competition with thousands of farm boys, and the company would give a college scholarship to five thousand of them who won. I raised a pig as a Lone Star farmer, and I got that scholarship.

Clyde came with me on the motorcycle to report to the Dean of Agriculture at Texas Tech in Lubbock. When we were close to campus, we got into a small accident with the bike, and I tore my jeans and scraped up my knee. I couldn't go all the way home to get cleaned up before I enrolled, because the dean was expecting me. So Clyde and I got back onto the motorcycle and kept my appointment with the dean.

As soon as he saw me, he asked what had happened. We told him about the motorcycle accident; so he got a first aid kit and patched me up. Then I got enrolled and got my scholarship all set. From that moment, the dean and I had a good working relationship.

While I was going to Texas Tech, I shoveled cow manure out of the college barns morning and night to earn my extra money for books and clothes and things. I'd have to go right from that job into class in the morning, and I wouldn't have time to change clothes or clean my boots off. So I'd get into the room, and the whole class would move away from me! At night I could go back and clean off my boots. I was not the most popular guy there.

I could go home on the weekends, because Plainview was close. Mother would wash my clothes on the weekends. That was nice for me! By that time she had a washing machine; so it was a little easier on her.

Home was only thirty miles away. I could hitchhike home. Back then, everybody hitchhiked everywhere.

During college, I think it was at spring break, I even made a bet with some of my classmates that I could get clear out to California hitchhiking. If I did, they had to pay my bus fare back. So I got the rides and made it to Los Angeles and called them! I had an aunt and uncle out there (Dad's brother, my uncle Fred and his wife), and they fed me and put me back on the bus.

You would think it would be a big change for me, living alone after being in a big family all my life. But first college and then the Air Force seemed like another big family to me.

I joined the Air Force in 1946 for three reasons. First, I loved my country and wanted to serve. Second, I wanted to fly airplanes, and the Army Air Force was the best way to achieve my goal. Third, I ran out of scholarship money for college!

There were benefits of being in the Air Force. I got to shower daily instead of bathing in a tin washtub once a week. The food was good, and I didn't mind the exercise and the orders. The Air Force was a pretty good deal for me. It was a lot of fun to be in the Army Air Force, which later (in 1947) became the U.S. Air Force.

Despite being on my own finally, I didn't have to care for myself in the way Mother had cared for me. I always ate at a cafeteria or the mess hall. And for laundry, I could take it to the BX or the cleaners on base. And after I was an officer, there was always the officer's club. I was single for a while.

I got an assignment when I was first learning to fly jet fighters out of South Carolina with one of the first jet squadrons. There was a young lady there I started seeing, and pretty soon we were engaged to be engaged. We were pretty serious and writing hot and heavy letters back and forth.

And then one day when I was going to combat in Korea, I got a "Dear John" letter from her. She had met somebody else that she wanted to start seeing instead. That whole experience made me bitter for a while. I stayed a bachelor for five years after she ended things. I dated a lot of girls, but I didn't find anyone else serious until I met Elaine.

I met her, and we got married three months later. I knew she was the right one. She was a beautiful, Swedish blonde, blue-eyed school teacher – just a wonderful, sweet person, and she loved the Air Force.

So I never did have to learn to do any of the housekeeping that my mother did!

I voted for the first time in 1952. I don't remember who I voted for, but I've always been a conservative and a Republican. Dad was as well, and so was Mother.

I remember when Lyndon Johnson was a young, gawky,

twenty or twenty-one year old kid running for Congress a long time ago. He came around politicking, and Daddy didn't like him at all.

He said, "That boy is going to cause this country a lot of trouble." And he did – he was not my favorite. He messed up the Vietnam War and caused a lot of people to get killed. I survived Vietnam, but I knew a lot of people who didn't make it.

Right after I voted the first time and before I married Elaine, I went home for Christmas in 1952. Our whole family's most memorable family reunion has to be the one in the letter Mother wrote. She really enjoyed that time together; we all did. It was the last time we were together just as siblings before any of us was married.

After that Christmas, we all scattered to the four winds.

Carl Glendon Schneider

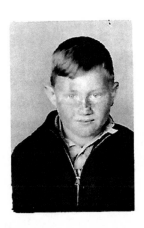

Chapter Seven (7)
Clyde Kerlin Schneider

I was born December 4, 1929, just in time to be Glen's accomplice and best friend. Mother must have seen right away that I took after her side of the family in looks and build. It's no mistake I have Kerlin for my middle name.

And in Farmer in the twenties, having the name Kerlin was an honor because of our Granddad Kerlin, who homesteaded there and was a pillar of the community. He liked having a Kerlin boy, and he and the aunts favored me a little. They'd take me along to visit them or other relatives or just to go get a treat. Mother would turn around and count noses, and I'd turn up missing!

Granddad Kerlin and Aunt Iris took me on a trip to Albuquerque, New Mexico when I was still very small, and before we left, we stopped by the Farmer store for gas and treats. Back then, you could get a box of peanuts that had a coin in it. Not every box had a coin, but the boxes with a coin might hold a penny, a nickel, a dime, or even a quarter. You never could tell until you opened it.

The man who owned the general store eventually became my uncle Alvin, but at the time of the Albuquerque trip, he was just sweet on Aunt Iris. He'd throw in some extra goodies just for her whenever she came by. And Uncle Alvin was really good at guessing the good boxes of peanuts with good coins; whether he could tell by shaking them or by judging the weight, he could get you a good box.

On the way to Albuquerque, I started eating a box of peanuts from Uncle Alvin's store. I was just sure that there was a quarter in that box. I was so excited. But my little stomach couldn't hold all of the peanuts; so I put the half-full box down on the seat. Well, Granddad liked to keep the car clean, and before I knew what he was doing, he'd grabbed that box and thrown it out the window!

So if any of you see a quarter by the side of the road on the way to Albuquerque – that's mine! That story reminds me of Uncle Tom throwing Mother's knife away with the apple peelings. Keeping things neat at all costs must have run in the Kerlin family.

When I was turning four, I got my first pair of long pants. They were pure white, just the color of vanilla ice cream – the only kind we ever made at home. I just loved them. I called them my ice cream britches. I brought them along on a trip with Granddad and Aunt Iris to see Aunt Bernice in Plains, TX, and I wore them on a Sunday morning, when we were all getting ready for church.

I was too busy and curious to stay inside and wait for the grownups to be finished getting ready. Besides, it was a big day

– my fourth birthday. I wanted to have fun. So I went outside, where I found an old bull inside a fence. He looked pretty interesting to me, and I went through the barbed-wire fence to see him up close. But he didn't want company, as he let me know pretty quickly.

Now, if you've ever been through a barbed wire fence, you know it's a lot easier to navigate when you're not scared and when you have plenty of time. I, on the other hand, was in a terrified rush when I was getting away from that bull. So I tore the ice cream britches and went howling to Aunt Iris. I can still remember standing on a stool in the kitchen while she stitched them up!

Being a Kerlin wasn't all trips and treats. It meant upholding the family legacy, too. Crosby County and the surrounding area had these celebrations once a year called the Old Settler's Reunion. The town built a shade out of poles and vines to make a kind of stage way out of town in Palo Duro Canyon. Then they had music and speeches and picnics and shows to celebrate the homesteaders and pioneers who had settled the land in the old days and paved the way for the rest of us.

One year, I got roped into playing Granddad Kerlin, while one of my girl cousins played Grandma Kerlin. We dressed up in old-fashioned clothes and pantomimed moving out west to Farmer. I didn't mind any of that part, but they wanted me to sing "Home on the Range."

Now, I'm no singer today, and I surely wasn't as a child, either. One of my elementary school teachers criticized my singing voice publicly, and it put me off trying to sing permanently. If the organizers were going to make me sing on stage, I'd just give up the whole thing as a bad job.

But Glen came to my rescue. We agreed between us that I'd dress up and act while he sang "Home on the Range" off stage. And that's just what we did.

At one of those Old Settler's Reunions, a man brought an airplane and sold rides in it. All of us kids went with Daddy to see the airplane, and we begged and begged for rides, though they were terribly expensive. We didn't get to go up, but I remember watching that airplane soar in the sky.

I was still pretty small when our part of Texas got electricity. It was a wonder being able to turn on a light or plug in a radio. Glen and I loved to listen to the radio.

Once, the folks went somewhere, maybe to town, and left Glen and me alone at the house. Daddy wanted some plowing done while he was gone; so he told us the section we were supposed to have done by the time he got back. We both said, "Yes, sir," and intended to have it done.

But that radio was calling to us. We took it up on the roof and listened to it for a while. It didn't seem like we had been listening for very long when we saw our car coming back up the road. We climbed back down as fast as we could and got right on that tractor! But Daddy knew what we had done and was not very pleased with us!

Glen and I helped a lot around the farm. We plowed and planted and hoed weeds and helped harvest when the time came. We did chores every morning, milking cows and feeding pigs and shoveling manure.

I helped Mother only occasionally inside, but more than the other boys. Once she asked me to help her hang wallpaper. You had to cut it just right, spread paste on the back with a brush, match it to the section already on the wall, and smooth out the bubbles that wanted to rise.

The room Mother wanted me to help her wallpaper had a slanting ceiling, and we were covering the slants. Hanging that paper was so tedious and so frustrating and so fiddly that I must not have been the most pleasant assistant she could have had. Soon Mother let me know that my help was no longer necessary.

But Glen and I both loved anything to do with machines. Mother used to wash clothes in an old washtub with lye soap and a scrub board. When she got her Maytag that operated with a foot crank, I kept it running for her. Glen and I both tinkered with the farm cars and tractors. And plowing wasn't so bad if you could use a tractor.

Daddy had grown up in a different era, and he was still more used to working with horses than machines. One time he was plowing with a tractor that had a wide front tire.

Daddy got too close to the barbed wire fence, and instead of turning the wheel, he started yelling, "Whoa! Whoa! Whoa!" at the tractor. Needless to say, the tractor paid him no mind. The barbed wire fence chewed his front tire to pieces before he could get it away. The whole thing was so funny to me that I just fell out laughing. Daddy was so mad that he chased me a good way across the field before he calmed down.

There was another time Daddy chased me across the fields for good reason. Glen and I were out on the county road, and a big boy called us over to his car and started talking to us. Naturally, we were flattered, and we rested our forearms on the sill of his car window. Inside, he pressed a button that sent a shock through us and made us jump away. I thought that was a pretty good trick.

The big boy showed me how he'd rigged the buzzer by connecting the coil from an old Model T Ford to a button. The driver was safe, because the seat insulated him from the charge. I couldn't wait to try it out.

I found a coil and installed it on the tractor. Then I waited my chance to pull the prank on Daddy. I called him over to the tractor, got up on the seat, and asked him to look at something on the drawbar. When I saw he had his hand planted on that metal, I pressed the button. After Daddy finished chasing me across the fields, he tore that whole contraption off the tractor. He wasn't as impressed by the buzzer as I was!

Daddy may not have preferred machines, but he could make them work. We had an old car that broke down from time to time, as all cars do, but we still took it on trips to Ralls and Lubbock regularly. After one trip to Lubbock, the fuel pump on that car went out.

Daddy and Glen and I worked together to figure out what was wrong. And then Daddy pointed out that the engine would still run if someone could work the fuel pump by hand. That's just what we did all the way home: we took turns lying on the front hood, dangling down, and working that fuel pump by hand!

Of course, all of us children liked it much better when we had something else on the front of the car – a block of ice. When my parents decided that we could have ice cream, Mother would get busy making the custard at home while Daddy went to town, bought a block of ice, wrapped it in burlap, and tied it to the front bumper. Then he would race home, hoping there would be enough ice left to make the ice cream!

Sometimes we had ice cream for First Friday nights, the times when the whole community gathered in the schoolhouse to create entertainment for ourselves. That entertainment might be an ice cream social, people playing music, a potluck dinner, or a school performance or a play. Those nights before anyone had television and when movies were rare were a lot of fun – they were a highlight of life on the farm.

The weather was bad for a good deal of my childhood, especially in the early springs, and the storms were scary to see. As we lived in Texas, the tumbleweeds dried and blew in the wind until they hit a fence. Then the dirt would pile onto the tumbleweed and the fence until the fences nearly disappeared.

When there was a terrible storm, we'd have to go to the cellar. I remember being awakened in the middle of the night to go across the yard and down into the cellar. And the cellar was dirty and dark and damp. I could just imagine snakes and spiders and other critters creeping out to get us while we huddled inside. I was almost more afraid of that cellar than the storms!

It was a good thing Mother could quote poetry to calm us down. She had quite a repertoire memorized, enough to relate to just about any occasion that arose.

Because of the weather ruining crops, often Daddy didn't grow enough feed for the animals. I remember herding our cows up the county roads during the summer to let them eat the roadside grass. When I was herding, I got to ride our horse, Jelly Bean, which was part farm horse and part pet.

We had a city cousin that none of us particularly liked, and we liked to play tricks on him. There was a shed on our property with an eave just about the height of Jelly Bean's saddle. We'd put the cousin on our horse, lead the horse under the eave, and get to laugh at our city cousin landing in horse manure.

Once he begged for a ride while we were way out on the road.

I guess he figured that there weren't any manure piles handy, and it would be safe to ride on the road. We put him up on Jelly Bean, but the saddle was loose. Our cousin fell right off to the ground, twisting the seat of the saddle so that it rested on Jelly Bean's stomach.

Jelly Bean didn't like that, and he didn't like the stirrups bothering his hooves. He took off for the house, kicking the saddle and stirrups to pieces along the way. We followed, but we were a lot slower than the horse.

Up at the house, Mother and our aunt saw Jelly Bean running for dear life with something dragging under his belly and tripping him. They were sure that a child was being dragged to death right before their eyes. Terrified, they ran at top speed to meet him. How relieved they were to see that the saddle was empty! For our part, we were sad to lose that saddle.

Glen and I decided that we needed some privacy, a place we could read or tell jokes or learn to smoke or tell stories all by ourselves or in the company of a few friends without any pesky sisters or parents following us. So we dug a cellar. The stairs down to it were really narrow on purpose to keep out parents. Daddy found an old metal Pepsi sign and made a roof for us so that the whole thing wouldn't collapse.

One day Grace had a friend over, and the girls wanted to ride bikes – the ones that belonged to Glen and me. We let our dear sister know that there was no way that was happening. However, when she went to discuss things with Mother, Glen and I figured that the cellar was as good a place as any to escape judgment until Grace's friend went home. So we hightailed it there.

Mother was too smart for us, though. She sat right down on the door of our play cellar and let us cool our heels there all afternoon while the girls rode our bikes as much as they liked. The girls even brought Mother her magazines and some cool drinks so that she wouldn't have to leave! When we emerged eventually, she meted out our punishment.

She used to cut switches from the peach tree for our whippings. I always used to say that she took a perfectly good tree down to a stump with those switches! We could always count on Mother to teach us right from wrong.

Mother allowed us from time to time to sell some extra eggs for money to get candy. We'd hide the eggs in the old church building to keep them safe until we could get to the general store, and then we'd retrieve our stash and exchange it for candy. Other kids in school did the same thing.

One day, Glen and I went to the old church and found some other kid's stash of eggs, and we took them to the general store to exchange for sweets just as if they'd been our own. We came home eating our bounty on a day Mother knew she had not given us any eggs to trade.

Mother cornered us, found out what we'd done, and marched us right back to Uncle Alvin to fess up and give our ill-gotten gain back in exchange for cash. Then we had to take the coins, find out which classmate had brought the eggs we stole, and give him what was his. That was a hard lesson – one that stuck with us for good.

Most of the time, though, when we got into mischief, we weren't doing anything wrong to anyone else – just amusing ourselves.

I remember one Halloween when we dragged a shock of grain out to the middle of the road and set fire to it to scare people on the road. And another Halloween, we crept through the fields to scare the storekeeper. But he saw us coming, crept around behind us, and scared us first! You've never seen two boys run for home as fast as Glen and I did that night.

For fun sometimes we'd build things around the farm. Once after we'd seen a rodeo, we decided to build a bronco chute. We wanted to test it for safety; so we put a calf inside and designated Finis as the cowboy. His bumps and bruises discouraged us from careers as bronco riders in the rodeo.

Another time, we had an old wagon, and we hitched a calf to it so that the calf could pull us along for a ride. But that calf somehow either got spooked or didn't like being pressed into service, because he went wild and tore through two or three barbed wire fences before we could get him stopped. That calf tore up our wagon, and he tore up the kids riding in the wagon, too!

When the wagon was ruined, we still had the runners. I'd heard stories of Granddad Kerlin moving the first store to Lubbock and moving his house to his homestead, and I'd seen houses moved around town. I decided to practice being a house mover using the runners of the old wagon.

We had an old chicken house, and I practiced house-moving with the old chicken house. That wasn't a problem. The problem was the coal shed, which I assumed no one needed anymore. I took it apart to use the lumber for runners.

Daddy came home later that day with a load of coal and found no place to put it. Guess who ended up working late into the night to rebuild that coal shed? Me!

The main crop Daddy grew on our land was cotton. Every step in the process of cultivating cotton is a chore and a bother. When it gets high enough, you've got to chop it, which means chopping the weeds out of it. That is a hot and thankless task.

One summer, Daddy set Glen and me a section of cotton to chop. "When you finish it," he told us, "you'll have it laid by for the summer." No more chopping – hooray! Glen and I worked hard and fast, and when we finished the last part of the last row, Glen banged his hoe against mine in a fit of jubilation – a fit that broke my hoe. Daddy was not thrilled.

When the cotton matured and burst into its white bolls, we picked it. The sharp plants cut our hands. And then we went with Daddy to the gin to have the seeds taken out and the bolls made into bales. The gin worked by steam power, and the waste water mixed with the earth outside to make what we called a slush pit – a wide expanse of mud.

Glen and I didn't want to waste our time in town standing around the gin; so we asked Daddy for some money. He gave us a nickel, and we ran toward town to spend it. But as we passed the slush pit, we dropped the nickel into it.

We spent all the time Daddy waited at the gin searching for that nickel. Part way through, we wanted to give up, and we asked Daddy for another nickel. But he had given us his last money. So we trudged back out and kept looking, with no success. When we arrived home, Mother was much more upset at the state of our clothes than the loss of the coin!

After Granddad Kerlin died, Daddy rented his house to a man named Peck Smith. He had a great sense of humor. Daddy would send us down to the old house to mill some corn, and while we were there, Peck would joke with us a while.

"How old are you boys?" he'd ask.

"Ten," I'd say, really quietly.

Peck would grin. "Why, I've got a daughter just your age! I

tell you what – when you're done here, you all come up to the house for a glass of iced tea and meet her."

Panicked at the prospect of solitary conversation with a girl, we'd say, "No, sir, I'm afraid we can't; Mother expects us home directly."

Peck thought that the whole routine was great fun.

He was a good man, though, and active in the church. There was a revival in 1943 at our church, and Peck Smith came and found Glen and me. "It's time you boys joined the church," he told us, and there was no joking around about the way he said it. That's when I was baptized. Peck Smith was an important factor in my decision.

For school, I attended the small schoolhouse in Farmer from 1934 to 1941. It had two classrooms and a small auditorium. I was not a good student. I failed sandbox, and they nearly took away my glue and scissors! When I graduated to using a fountain pen, the teacher nearly had to use a raincoat to walk by my desk.

We had a cloakroom in the front of the school where we'd all keep our lunches. There was a stray cat at one time that would get into the cloakroom while we were all working and eat our lunches.

The principal sent the older boys to kill it. They took the cat out back and thought they'd killed it and buried it. But we'd come back from a class and find that old cat still lurking around. The boys had only stunned it instead of killing it.

Finally the principal had had enough. At lunch time, he went home and got his shotgun, and he took the stray cat to the back of the schoolhouse. We heard two shots – blam! blam! – and we never saw that cat again.

At recess, we used to play baseball. I can remember one baseball game when I was playing center field. I felt something uncomfortable on my legs. I looked down and discovered that I was standing on a red ant hill! I ran for the outhouse, stripping off my clothes along the way to get those ants out!

But sometimes we'd have a baseball competition with some of the other rural schools. We'd go over to the other school, or they would come to us. Then we'd spend the afternoon playing. It was a fun afternoon when we could take part in those games.

One really dramatic event happened at Farmer school while we were there. A man named Eric Hilliard had a motorcycle, and for whatever reason, he decided to ride it over the see-saws outside the school. The kids crowded around the windows to see him.

He did all right for a while, but then he started going faster and faster to amuse the kids. Suddenly, he fell off, hit his head, and lay still. We all wanted to go outside and see the dead body, but the teachers made us stay inside. Eventually Eric came to and rode home.

As soon as we came home from school, we did more farm work. If we were out in the fields, we carried a crockery jug of water wrapped in wet burlap to keep it cool. We used a corncob for the stopper.

If we were drinking at the well, we used a gourd dipper. Gourd plants grew that turned hollow inside when they dried. We'd cut them in half lengthwise so that the neck of the gourd was the handle, while the round part held the water. We made sure to drink while we worked, because it got really hot outside.

Once Daddy had us plow some weeds that had gotten out of control and grown higher than the tractor. They were so high that they covered the radiator. Daddy sent us with two buckets of water to refill that boiling radiator while we worked.

Well, we cut down those weeds and refilled the radiator. Then we cut more weeds and refilled the radiator again. We cut more weeds, and we were out of water. But we knew that just one more pass with the tractor would finish the work. We didn't want to go all the way back to the house just for one bucket of water!

Like I said, we'd been drinking plenty of water while we worked. Now we figured that we could use all that water we'd been drinking to save us a trip. So Glen and I both peed into the radiator. Then we finished cutting weeds and put the tractor away.

The next time Daddy used the tractor, it smelled to high heaven. Daddy wondered and wondered what in the world had happened to stink up his farm equipment. It wasn't until years later that we finally confessed!

I didn't generally help with Mother's work (besides fixing the washing machine), but I did help in her garden occasionally. Once she let me have a whole row of potatoes to plant and raise myself. I was proud of those potatoes.

We had neighbors, Mr. and Mrs. Tom Reed, whom I liked. Mrs. Reed came by to visit Mother once, and while the two of them were walking in the garden, Mrs. Reed complimented my potatoes. I was so pleased that I immediately dug the whole row and presented them to her. Not a one of them was as big as a hen's egg. I could fit the entire crop in a coffee can. But she was touched.

I did some work for the Reeds, plowing and driving a culti-vator and such. I liked to sleep over there. Once when I worked for them, they took me to town and to the fair. They were really nice people.

I mentioned how much Glen and I liked machines. When we were twelve and thirteen, we bought Clayton Thornton's 38 Harley Davidson motorcycle. 38 wasn't the year; it was the model, the one with a standard frame and one cylinder. Glen went on his bicycle to buy it and learn to ride it, and then he came back to teach me. We took turns riding the tractor and practicing the motorcycle.

Then we put the motorcycle down on a sheet, took the whole thing apart down to the last bolt and washer, and put it back together. We both knew enough about it to know what needed fixing, and to fix what needed fixing. We rode that motorcycle everywhere around town. Some of the neighbors thought we'd never live to be grown!

That same summer, we traded in the 38 for a 61 overhead valve, 2 cylinder model. It was so big that it took us both to ride it. One of us had to jump off and put down the kickstand when we stopped, even at traffic signals.

It was a good thing we were both able mechanics, because the motorcycle did break down. When we couldn't fix it, we'd have to get Daddy to fetch it with the car and trailer. But we were allowed a great deal of independence.

When we were still young teens, we took that motorcycle across the state to Mansfield, near Fort Worth, to visit the Goodes, old friends of ours. The cops did stop us once, and we had to convince them that we owned the bike and were allowed to be out on it. Other than that stop, we rode that bike for a thousand miles that summer with no accidents!

We learned that we had to look out for our bike, though.

When we went to Ralls and left the bike outside a store or a business, the big boys would gather around and try to take it for rides without even asking – some of them might have wanted just to take it for good. So we learned to take a few parts out of the bike to keep them off it.

Glen and I also bought a Model A Ford together that we could use to get around. There was gas rationing during the war years, though; so getting anywhere far required some planning. Farmers were allowed extra gas to run tractors and farm machinery. One of us would tell Daddy that we were going to Ralls and distract him while we took enough gas for a round trip to Lubbock.

When our family moved to Plainview, Glen and I brought our motorcycle with us, and we'd ride it to school. In fact, when we first moved to town, we lived in the small dairy barn on the farm Daddy had bought and took ourselves to school. We felt very grown up and independent.

One weekend when Daddy went home to see Mother and the other children, I went away for some reason and left Glen at that dairy with a friend. When I got back, every pot and pan we owned was full of gravy! Glen and his friend had tried to make gravy, but they'd get it too thick and try to thin it out. Then it would be so thin that they'd try to thicken it up! Glen must have made gallons of gravy that day.

Some of the kids saw us riding the motorcycle and wanted turns. Glen soon cured them of that wish. He could zig zag and almost lay that bike down on either side without crashing. He'd take a kid on the back of the bike, zig zag a while, and then ride with the front tire of the motorcycle under the back of the school bus. Few who rode with him once ever asked for a second ride.

Glen and I made friends with other boys who lived on small farms or whose families had just come from the country. One of our friends was Junior Wells. He took us on kind of a boy's weekend to Lubbock, and he drove his car on the wrong side of the highway underpass. It scared us pretty well.

Once Junior had us all over to his house when his parents were away. We got out his tractors, which worked with a hand brake, and we started playing around with them in the orchard, acting almost like we were jousting.

We'd get those tractors going right at one another with one boy steering and another working the hand brake in the back. It was a game of nerve to see who would be the last to turn away or work the hand brake to get his tractor to swerve away from the other one. One boy hit his brake too late, and that tractor went straight up the side of a tree and over.

Luckily, the driver and the brake man jumped off in time to avoid being hurt. But I'm afraid we all went home and left Junior to his fate. I didn't envy him explaining that upside-down tractor to his folks.

I got to be a much better student in high school. I enrolled in DO – diversified occupations. So I took academic courses until lunch, and then I spent the afternoon learning trades. I was in the program for two years, spending one year in auto mechanics and the other in the electrical shop. I've always had a knack for fixing things, a knack that came in handy for DO. By the time I was in high school, I was even invited to join the National Honor Society.

When I lived in Plainview, I got summer jobs with the farmers just out of town. I got my own plow, and I'd hire myself out to do plowing work fast. I'd even sleep in the fields and plow by moonlight when the moon was bright enough.

In high school I had a great desire to learn to fly. It might have been connected to the fact that Glen was learning to fly in the Army Air Force just then. I went to the airfield in Plainview and talked to the owner, James Miller, about maybe taking flying lessons. He looked over at me and said, "Let's start right now!" I did.

After only two hours in the air, I had my first solo. I botched the landing; so my instructor told me to try again. I tried four more times before I stuck it.

According to my log book, my first flight was on March 3, 1946. My first solo was on March 19, just a few weeks later. I graduated high school in the spring of 1946, and then I got my pilot's license on December 20, 1946.

My first passenger was Charles Bowen, who was a friend from school, and the second, of course, was Glen. My third passenger was J.C. Webb, another school friend, and the fourth was Margaret Clayborn. She lived a little ways out of town, and I used to land in one of her father's fields to pick her up and take her for a ride. Speaking as a parent now, I'm sure her parents were thrilled.

When I was still pretty new to flying, an aerial photographer named Lewis Wimberley hired me to take him up so that he could shoot aerial photos of the wheat harvest. We had to fly low to get the angles he needed, and I found that I liked flying low.

I was flying an Aeronca Champion, which was the first airplane marketed to civilians after World War II. The manufacturer wanted to advertise that it was so easy to learn that a boy could fly it. The company learned from James Miller that I was flying the Champion, and company representatives sent a newspaper photographer to snap my picture in cowboy boots getting out of the plane. A national flying magazine ran that picture.

The flying industry and city councils wanted to boost the growing airplane industry. They held Flying Farmer's Breakfasts across the state and gave away prizes to encourage flying farmers to attend. There were prizes for the oldest, flier, the youngest flier, the one who'd traveled the farthest to attend, and so forth.

I went to several of them, and that summer, I could pretty much guarantee that I'd win the prize for the youngest pilot every time. Then another young pilot started showing up. He was a month younger than me; so he took all the prizes from then on!

A friend of mine flew a two-cylinder plane to one of these breakfasts in Clarendon, Texas. When we were getting ready to leave, the headwind was really strong, but he decided to fly against it. He flew for three hours and barely got out of town. Finally he had to land where he'd started, call a friend to pick him up, and drive back on a calmer day to pick up his plane.

I enrolled in Texas Tech in 1947 and studied business. I definitely wasn't interested in studying agriculture. While I attended college, I kept flying.

In the summer of 1947, I flew some with Leonard Wittkoski. He'd washed out of the Army flying cadets, and he never got over the disappointment. So he bought the same plane just to prove he could fly it. He was a crazy man in the air. He'd fly low over sheep herds and buzz them to watch them scatter. I always felt sorry for the poor shepherds that had to gather them back up.

While I was a college student, I flew a friend and his girlfriend home for a visit. The airfield close to his home was hard to locate, and the landing strip was short. I had to try three times to land.

I was so busy flying that I didn't notice the state of my passengers. When I turned around, I saw that the girlfriend was scared to death, and my friend didn't look much better. He paid me for the trip and told me that they'd take the bus home!

I did help the flying instructor at the college airfield teach students to read maps and match them to the terrain. I'd go up with the student and copilot while he flew. One tech student got on with empty suitcases, landed in a shady place, and filled his suitcases with bootleg liquor.

I was shocked and worried. He was overloading the plane, putting our fuel calculations way off, and what's worse, he was breaking the law. Once we landed and he got off my plane, I decided I was done instructing college students. I heard later in life that the bootlegger kept going the same way and ended up about like you'd expect.

In the summer of 1947, I took a car trip to Durango, CO with my friends Russell Crocker and J.C. Webb and J.C.'s parents, Mr. and Mrs. Webb. To get from Plainview to Durango, we spent $19.91 on gasoline and $1.70 on four quarts of oil. It came to $21.61 for the whole trip. Can you imagine spending that today?

I still came home pretty often on breaks from school while I attended college. On one break in August of 1949, I even brought Glen with me to Muleshoe, TX for a Flying Farmer's

CHAPTER EIGHT (8)
Finis (Frank) Earl Schneider

I guess the first thing that has always been a concern is my name. I don't remember that my parents ever told me where they got the name Finis. In recent years I have learned that it was the middle name of Jefferson Davis, the president of the confederacy - that is Jefferson Finis Davis. Perhaps this is the answer.

When I was in the Army in 1952 in Fort Monmouth, my boss, Captain Boyle, gave me the name Frank. I go by that name except with my brothers and sisters. Most people know me as Frank; my wife calls me Frank.

My memories of the years at Farmer are not necessarily in chronological order. A really early memory concerns a shower that Mother was giving someone. My cousin Wanda and I were supposed to come around the corner carrying a basket full of gifts, but I got embarrassed and didn't want to go through with it. I don't remember how that turned out.

Mother used to have quilting parties. So we had a quilting

frame in our living room that she'd raise up near the ceiling when it wasn't in use, and when some women would come to sew and gossip, they would lower that frame down to sitting level. And then they'd sit there and sew and talk.

I spent a lot of time with my brothers and sisters; I was sort of in the middle of them. Glen and Clyde were a pair. They were pals and had the motorcycle. I think sometimes I told on them, and that got me in trouble. But I don't remember any great conflict with them.

I thought Clyde was pretty humorous, and so was Joyce. So I mentally paired them in that temperament. And I thought of Grace and Glen as instigators. JoAnn was just cute. We all liked to entertain her.

We had a riding horse named Jelly Bean; a collie dog whose name was Tillie, I think; and two big farm horses named Sam and Ben. Sam and Ben were humongous. They were a lot bigger than Jelly Bean was. They had big old hooves like big Clydesdales – the ones on the commercials. They were just impressive to me, and they were strictly to pull the plows. I don't remember ever riding them.

I do remember having chores such as milking cows, chopping cotton, pulling cotton, and the like. Our land ran right up across the road from the store and gas station at Farmer, and one time when we were chopping cotton, I got sick at my stomach. My dad gave me a nickel and let me go over to the store and buy a Coke to settle my stomach. I think that was the first Coke I ever drank.

I did not like pulling cotton - we pulled it rather than picked it. The difference was that we pulled the bolls with cotton, and then it was separated at the gin. I always got my hands all scratched up, and the bags were heavy to drag around. But the good part was when the wagon was full of cotton and on the way to the gin. We would ride on the top of the cotton to the gin and then play on the bales of cotton stacked in the gin yard.

Our dad built a blacksmith shop up by the store, school, and gin. I went to get my bicycle out of that shop one time when it was closed. I tried to crawl in a back window, and the log I was standing on rolled away. The window I had raised came down on my neck, and I was left hanging. I started yelling, and the lady who lived in the house on the gin yard heard and saw me and came and rescued me.

Once I was given a pig to raise, and I entered it in the county fair. I was always proud to announce that it won third place. What I didn't want to say was that there were only three pigs entered!

We had a lot of dust storms in those days, and they were scary to me. You could see them coming, and everything would turn dark when they rolled through. Also, we had some heavy snows. I remember once the snow was so high you could step right over the clothesline.

Many times on Saturdays I would go over to Granddad Kerlin's to spend the night with him. On Sunday morning, he would read the comics to me and insert my name in place of one of the characters. Out in the pasture near his house, there was a mound we always thought might contain some Indian relics, but we were never allowed to dig it up.

I think when Granddad got older he moved in with Aunt Iris and Uncle Alvin. He died at Aunt Iris's, and I remember that I saw him in the casket and went outside and cried. Someone came out and tried to comfort me. Also, it rained so hard I could not go to his funeral in Ralls. In fact, they had to have a tractor pull the hearse to the cemetery. After Granddad Kerlin died, we moved over to his house and lived there a while.

I remember on Sunday evenings, Mother would get out the family Bible and let us select favorite Bible stories for her to read to us. I don't remember all of those stories, but I do remember that the David and Goliath story was a favorite. When we lived at our granddad's house, we'd sit out on the front porch in the early evenings to read those stories, because we didn't have Sunday evening church services.

Also, Mother had some good, useful sayings. She would say, "If at first you don't succeed, try, try again." I heard that a million times. And also, I really heard this one often: "Two wrongs don't make a right." She taught us a lot; she was sort of our sage, I guess. She liked poetry; we used to hear poems, too, from her.

Mother didn't get too excited about anything, though. I remember when Pearl Harbor happened. It was one Sunday morning when Mother was ironing. We had a little white radio. I remember listening to the radio with her and hearing the announcement that Pearl Harbor had been bombed. Mother just kept on with her work.

Another example of how calm and steady she was happened one time when the boys were riding the horse. The saddle got turned around on them, and a neighbor who was watching got all excited with Mother and wondered if the boys were hurt. Mother said, "Well, when the horse gets here, we'll find out." That was sort of the way she dealt with problems.

Of course, school took up a lot of my childhood years. I guess we had a fairly typical rural school for the times. There were three classrooms and an auditorium. We used the same building for school and for church.

We did not have a full-time minister. There were ministers who took turns coming to Farmer. A man named Jeff Reed always led the singing, and someone played the upright piano. Our cousin Harold Vernon got paid a quarter each week during the winter to go start a fire in the auditorium for church, and sometimes I would help.

The school had a water fountain out in the playground and outhouses: one for boys and one for girls. At the end of the eighth grade, we had a party, and we paired up as boy and girl dates. My date was Janice Irvin. We got dressed up, and we were taken to Ralls, where we had dinner at a restaurant and then went to see a movie. As I recall, the name of the movie was *DuBarry Was a Lady* starring Lucille Ball.

I guess it was at the start of my eighth grade that our parents decided to move to Plainview. I think Grace was in college, and Daddy and Glen and Clyde went on to Plainview to get our house ready. Mother, Joyce, JoAnn, and I moved into a little house on the gin yard. I think we stayed so that the three of us could finish the school year at Farmer.

One time during this stay Marlin Sawyer and I rode horses over to the canyon past Cone and played cowboys and Indians all day. We had known the Sawyers a long time; they were neighbors that lived over near Cone. Marlin was a little older than me. He was more in Clyde's age group. But since Glen and Clyde had already gone to Plainview, he went with me to the canyon. That was a fun day.

When it was time for our family to move to Plainview, I was given the job of riding our horse to the new house. I started out early and got to the little town of Petersburg by lunch time. I found a farm machine of some kind near the one cafe and tied the horse there while I got a hamburger for lunch. Then I started out again. After about three miles, I got tired of riding and got off and led the horse. Pretty soon Daddy and Clyde came along in the car, and Clyde took over the riding of the horse. I got to go on in the car with Dad.

About my dad – I think about the greatest thing he did for all of us was give us his genes. Look at all six of us still going! And I think that must have come from my dad. He lived to be ninety-four. Mother died early; so I assume that the longevity came down through my dad, the best I can tell.

Our house in Plainview was at 24th and Independence. We had about ten acres of land, a barn, and an outhouse. There was an upstairs sort of attic where we boys were assigned.

During my high school days, I enjoyed history class and woodworking shop. My favorite teacher was Mrs. Mead Griffin. She taught English. I also remember spending time at school with Carol Mitchell and Eugene Watson. But I was really interested in sports. I wrote a sports column in the high school paper, and the title of my column was "Finish with Finis."

I did get a letter for A-squad basketball. The most points I ever scored in a game was ten. I played some B-squad football and was one of the managers of the A-squad team. One time during the halftime of a game, the coach was making a big speech to get the team fired up, and in the middle of it I dropped a tape can on the concrete floor. It made a big noise. The coach looked at me and said, "Schneider, did you have to do that?"

Mother taught in the school for Seth Ward (a suburb of Plainview), and I offered to coach their football team. We only played one game against another school in Plainview, and we lost that six to nothing. So that was a short coaching career for me. We didn't play any more games.

During the summers, I worked at various jobs. I cleaned engine parts at a repair shop; I bagged groceries at a grocery store; and I worked as a bell hop and elevator operator at the Hilton hotel. My biggest job was working in the wheat harvest in the summer with Clyde.

A man named Leonard Wittkoski had two combines, two trucks, and a small airplane. He would fly ahead of Clyde and me and get contracts, and we would bring the equipment on the trucks. The first time I drove a combine, I failed to keep the elevator high enough and plowed into a terrace. Otherwise, I did very well. We would start in East Texas and work our way north, usually ending in Denver, Colorado. One time we cut the wheat around the runways at the Denver airport.

I used to fly with Leonard sometimes in his little airplane. He'd take off from these pastures, and though I'd swear he wasn't going to clear the fence at the end, he always did. In fact, I wasn't a big flier to begin with. You can tell that Clyde and Glen both ended up in the Air Force, and I went to the Army. So I was the black sheep in the family because I didn't take to flying very well.

Back at home, I would go to the movies on Saturday night and then stop in the drugstore and have a pineapple sundae. I only had one date in high school, and that was to the senior prom. My date was Peggy Smith, and after the prom we went to a party at the home of the president of Wayland College. I don't remember how that came about.

I started to college at West Texas State in Canyon in the fall of 1948, when I was sixteen. I went up there early to help get the dorms ready, and my parents drove me up there and dropped me off. I remember hating to see them drive away, because there were almost no other people at the college that early. When they left, I bought a Mounds candy bar and went to my room.

On weekends, I would get out on the highway and hitchhike home. Then on Sunday afternoons, I would get back out on the highway and get a ride back to Canyon. I was a speech major, and I got a job giving a sports report on a radio station in Amarillo. I would hitchhike up there in the afternoon and do the show about 9:00 PM and then hitchhike back to Canyon.

In the middle of my junior year, the Korean War had started, and I quit school and enlisted in the army. I guess this was when I left home, though I still came home for holidays when I could.

When I graduated from OCS at Fort Monmouth, New Jersey, Glen came up there for the graduation. We took a cargo plane to some little town in Texas and caught the bus from there back home. But we were just sitting crammed in these little bucket seats on the sides of this cargo plane. For someone who already didn't like to fly, it wasn't too much fun.

I was still assigned to Fort Monmouth during Mother's happiest Christmas in 1952. I found another person who was going somewhere else; I forget where he was headed, just somewhere down that way. We shared the driving, and we drove all night, it must have been fifty-two hours, to get home.

It was just great to be there. And I think that's the time we went to church, all three of us boys, in uniform. So we really enjoyed having that experience.

.

CHAPTER NINE (9)
Launa Joyce Schneider Johnson-Winn

I'VE always said that if you were the only survivor of an event or period of time, the way you told it was the way it was! But when you have five siblings who were there, you'd better try to be factual.

So…I think my earliest memory was of being placed in the middle of a bed so that I could hold my new baby sister, JoAnn, who was born in 1937 when I was nearly three. I always thought the baby got more attention than I did. She was little and cute (with dimples!) and seldom got into trouble.

When I was about four years old, I recall a trip to Albuquerque, New Mexico (a place where I eventually spent twenty-eight years). I had a new lavender dress, and I rolled down a hill in Roosevelt Park wearing it – getting grass stains along the way. I got a paddling.

Later, I seem to recall sitting in a wagon under our big round dining table as we were moving to Granddad Kerlin's farm. That would have been in 1941, when I was seven. When I hear the word "home," I often think of Granddad's place, though we must have only lived there two or three years.

One night when I had trouble sleeping, I mentally reconstructed his farm. I could remember at least eleven outbuildings, which made it a fascinating place for a child. There were a large barn, harness shed, well house, smoke house, shelters for chickens and pigs and cows, a car shed, a shack for hired workers, and several others.

Of course, we also had a storm cellar. Instead of a detailed weather report on a TV, we had Daddy saying, "I don't like the looks of that cloud!" Then we'd all troop down the stairs and wait until he said the danger had passed.

I don't remember the Dust Bowl storms, because I was too young to remember when the worst of them hit. Since that time, I've seen a storm nearly as bad. But the Dust Bowl wasn't a vivid memory for me.

While we were living at Granddad's house, I finally got a bicycle (and could quit pestering a neighbor boy about riding his). I also spent a lot of time riding an old work horse named Buck.

Music has always been important to me, though we might have owned only one vinyl record, "Down Yonder," with flip side "Back Up and Push." Around the time we moved to Granddad's house, an old pump organ was left with us. I became obsessed with trying to play it. Somehow, our parents managed to afford piano lessons for me, and I started piano lessons at Cone, which was about five miles away.

One week I was allowed to ride my bicycle to my lesson, meeting another piano student along the way. Afterward, I decided there was no rush to get home. So I had lunch at the other student's home ... stopped by the schoolhouse where an aunt was involved with rehearsal for a play … and continued to chat with a cousin.

Mother and my oldest brother finally tracked me down – on a motorcycle – and to put it mildly, Mother was not pleased. I was in deep trouble. Unfair! After all, I was already nine years old.

And music was responsible for one other problem. The manager of the local cotton gin had a fine bass voice, and he often sang at community gatherings. I thought that he was just wonderful. Unfortunately, he died during the time that I had measles.

Mother said I cried and cried and begged to see him before they buried him. Afraid that I would make myself even sicker, Mother arranged the visit. Children visiting in that home had to be taken elsewhere. I was wrapped warmly in a quilt and taken to see him.

I vaguely recall my first public musical performance. Though I'd only had piano lessons for a short while, I was asked to play at Sunday school. I blundered my way through "Trust and Obey," and one of the deacons prayed for me. I'm sure I needed it!

Despite my love of music, I lived in mortal dread of piano recitals, which came far too often. Mother, being musically inclined, seemed proud of my efforts. She often asked me to play something when she had a visitor – then they'd talk through the whole piece.

I think that Mother's life as a farm wife and mother was pretty difficult. I recall her as always being busy with cooking, sewing, laundry, cleaning, and all the other work that went into keeping us clean and fed.

When we lived on the farm, JoAnn and I were young enough

that we didn't have many chores. We were responsible for carrying in coal for the heating stove, and I know that we gathered eggs.

When JoAnn started school, Mother had the opportunity to return to teaching, which I believe made her life much easier. I remember being so impressed that we now had our ironing done by someone else!

Despite how busy she always seemed, she generally had a cheerful outlook. She tended to find some of our childish nonsense amusing, though she might put her hand over her mouth and say, "Oh, I shouldn't laugh at that!" She often commented on beautiful sunsets, colorful flowers, and lovely music. She sang sometimes while she worked, and I've realized most of the songs were either Irish or Scottish.

And one of her favorite things was memorizing poetry. I remember one winter when she read *Snowbound* to us. She was occasionally asked to do public readings.

She always wore dresses or jumpers – and hose. For church, you could be sure she'd have on a hat and gloves, at least after we moved to town.

All of us are amazed to recall that she never raised her voice to us, often only expressing her disappointment if we misbehaved. If needed, we did get paddlings, though.

Whereas our mother was affectionate and outgoing, Daddy was reserved and didn't show much emotion. The main times that I observed him being emotional were when Mother was ill or had an injury of some sort. Daddy's mother had died at a fairly young age, and he was raised by a stern German father.

When JoAnn and I were small, I can remember Daddy holding us in his lap while we made little curls in his hair. Later,

I recall that hugging him was sort of like hugging a tree – he didn't relax at all. But in many ways, like what he did for us and the advice he gave to us, we realized that he did love us.

It seems as though we were related to a large number of our neighbors, so there was a lot of visiting back and forth. Sunday afternoons were usually spent visiting someone. If there weren't children in the home, I recall being expected to sit quietly while the adults discussed crops and politics and other boring subjects.

We regularly attended Sunday school and church, held in the schoolhouse. There was usually no question about attending church – we all went! Preaching was by different denominations. I especially liked dinner on the grounds held sometimes after church.

However, Mother loved picnics and was known to say on occasion, "God gave us this beautiful day to enjoy. Let's go on a picnic." I recall several trips to the rugged Caprock area or to Palo Duro Canyon.

We always said a blessing at meals, and Mother frequently read the Bible to us. She used Bible quotations to try to influence our behavior – we really hated that. Daddy wasn't outspoken about religion, but it was apparent it was important to him. And he never did unnecessary chores on Sunday. Thanks to Mother and Daddy setting an example for us, all six of us are church members, and I'm sure where everyone is on Sunday morning.

In Farmer, there was a monthly Community Night, with music by neighborhood fiddlers and guitar players. I particularly remember the Tom Reeds, who didn't have children. They were especially attentive to all us kids, and the yearly Easter egg hunt was held in their pasture. The Farmer community was very close; I lost some of that sense of belonging when we moved to town.

I still remember fondly my first grade teacher, Eleanor Hayes, though she did scold me once for telling that one of the boys poured water in the sand box. One of my favorite friends was Vera Kinkler, although I was jealous of her nice clothes. Once I lied to the teacher at health check that Vera's ears were dirty.

I think that my siblings and I probably rode the bus to school most years. At recess, we played jacks or hopscotch in the sandy school yard. I loved workbooks and always wanted to do more than the day's assignment.

Grace went away to college when I was about nine; so I don't recall much about the time she lived at home. I do remember that we three girls always shared a bedroom. Because JoAnn and I were afraid to go to bed in a dark room, Mother would ask Clyde to lie across the foot of our bed until Grace came to bed. She had a fear of someone under the bed grabbing her leg, and I recall Clyde doing so one time and sending Grace into hysterics.

Our move to Plainview when I was ten opened a whole new world for me. Life in Plainview introduced me to movies (picture shows), a swimming pool, much more skilled piano teachers, and the public library system. For only ten cents a month, I could borrow all the books I could carry.

When we lived out in the country, Daddy socialized with most of the community farmers. After we moved to town, he had less in common with the residents. He didn't cope well with change and routines unfamiliar to him.

When he was home during the day, he usually picked me up

from the high school for lunch. The principle thing I remember his cooking was breaded tomatoes. I don't know whether he really liked them or if that was one dish he knew how to make.

Growing up with three older brothers hasn't always been easy. They seemed to feel that girls should be their slaves.

For instance, since our house in Plainview had a second story, the oldest brother (who shall remain nameless) would ask me to run upstairs and get his shoes or something. "If you can get back before I count ten, I'll give you a nickel," he'd promise. When I'd return, he'd be counting, "Eleven, twelve ... boy, you almost made it that time."

Glen was somewhat cocky and self-confident, but fun and full of ideas. I think he was usually the one who dreamed up adventures that got himself and other siblings in hot water. Clyde was usually inventing something or tackling a new project or hobby. He was also probably the most soft-hearted toward us girls.

Clyde, who was interested in electronics, built a crystal radio set. Then he advanced to a home broadcasting station, FLOP, which would reach about two miles. I could play hymns on it for an elderly neighbor. And there was Finis' famous commercial, "For a better butter buy, buy Betsy's better butter."

Finis, who was younger than the other boys, was somewhat of a loner. He was the only boy interested in sports, and he became a manager for the high school football team. Though a bit shy, he was quite nice looking and caught the attention of numerous girls.

When I was still exploring the new joys of Plainview, Grace was already in college at West Texas State in Canyon. JoAnn and I were allowed to ride the train there one weekend to visit her. My clearest memory of the trip was of Sunday morning breakfast in the dining hall. The tables were set with crisp, white cloths … and I spilled my tomato juice all over ours!

In town, since Mother was often busy with teaching details or taking more college courses, I became mother's little helper, taking over much of the cooking. That job has remained one of my favorite activities. It always irritated us girls that the boys weren't expected to do any chores around the house. I think that Grace did work in the fields when needed.

After we moved to Plainview, JoAnn and I attended a country school where Mother taught. I made a number of good friends and was valedictorian of my junior high class (where there were only seven graduates). Also, in the eighth grade, I became the reporter for my 4-H club. The first time I saw one of my reports in the local newspaper, I was hooked on writing. So the written word has always been one of my passions.

High school was more of a challenge, especially because I was only twelve years old. It helped to know I had older brothers in the same building. I met Sally Moore while we were registering, and we remained friends for years. Kenneth Rodgers was my seatmate in journalism class. We laughed so much that the teacher threatened to throw us out.

That teacher was Elinor Griffin, who was also the assistant principal. She probably influenced me more than any other teacher. After I left Plainview, I made a point of visiting her when I was back in town.

Being a grandchild of John Kerlin carried a lot of weight in the home county, but no one knew Granddad or was impressed by our lineage in town. So we had to establish our own identity there. Several of my classmates had dads who were doctors, professors, or lawyers, and I think that intimidated me a bit. Nevertheless, I joined every club that interested me and competed in several positions.

So far as life at home, of course, there were fewer chores to be done. We did operate a small dairy for a time, which involved different activities. Eventually, we moved to a more urban part of town.

Guess what impressed me most there? ICE! We had a refrigerator and could have all the ice we wanted. I think that's why I still fill my glass to the top with ice when I drink something cold.

As several other siblings did, I finished high school at sixteen. After finishing high school in 1950, I went to stay with my sister, Grace, who was teaching in Albuquerque. Again I became hooked: on Albuquerque.

I got a job as a file clerk for a heavy equipment company, but had to be emancipated in order to earn my own income at that age. By the time I was seventeen, I had my own little basement apartment near downtown. Mother, especially, had always encouraged us to be independent and adventuresome; so it seemed quite natural to do so.

I don't recall being particularly lonely, though I think I called home fairly often. I enjoyed the space, freedom, and privacy after living amid such a large family. I worked as a file clerk until entering in the University of New Mexico the next year as a journalism major.

Unfortunately, I didn't apply myself to studies the second year, and I dropped out under academic probation. I worked for the *Albuquerque Journal* for about a year afterwards. I also wrote for the *Ralls Banner* not long after that.

Incidentally, thirty-five years later when I again enrolled at UNM, I was informed that I was still under academic probation! This time, after I'd completed 26 hours of studies with a 4.0 average, I was invited to join an honor society.

My most memorable story about my relationship with Mother occurred after I left home. At twenty-two, I was engaged and planning an ill-advised marriage. Despite her reservations, Mother finally told me that I should go ahead and marry if I felt that it was right for me. "Otherwise, you might regret it the rest of your life," she said. I know she was relieved when I decided against the marriage.

I also felt Daddy's care and concern after I was officially away from home. When I was grown and working for a small weekly paper, Daddy went with me to look for a car. He would comment to the salesmen, "My daughter is trying to decide between going to Linotype school in New York and buying a car." Not that the salesmen cared! And after I left home, he wrote me two letters – one urging me to work closer to home, and one advising against a proposed marriage. So I knew that my welfare mattered to him.

I think that we all feel fortunate to have grown up with good parents in a Christian home. And we all stay in touch and enjoy getting together.

Chapter Ten (10)
JoAnn Virginia Schneider Lamb

I was born on Sunday morning, February 21, 1937. We were all born at home. That's something that you don't hear about very often anymore, unless it's an emergency.

When I was born, Mother and Daddy didn't have a first name settled for me. They had a middle name, Virginia, after my Grandmother Schneider: Elizabeth Virginia Bare Schneider. They just didn't know which first name they were going to put with it.

I made six children under ten for my parents, and I'm sure my mother never expected to have six. They just weren't prepared for me. A neighbor lady had heard that I was born and came down the road to see me, and they asked her what I ought to be called. She said JoAnn, and that was my name.

When I was very small, my brothers put me in a washtub in the middle of the horse tank. I was only two or three, and I thought that the water was a hundred feet deep. My brothers

141

just stood off and laughed; they knew I wasn't in any danger and didn't realize how terrified I was. I'm still afraid of water to this day because of that stunt. I think they got a whipping for pulling it; at least, I hope they did!

Another time, Glen put me in a barrel on a sled and hooked the sled to the drawbar of the tractor. When he went through a gate, the barrel tipped, and I hit my head on the drawbar of the tractor. I had to go into town to have my head sewn up, though I have no recollection of the actual stitches.

All I remember is that my Daddy took me to the drugstore and got me an ice-cream cone. I had never had one before. I remember thinking that I was the only one who got ice cream and that everyone else had to stay home without ice cream because I had gotten my head split open.

One of the earliest memories I have is of Granddad Kerlin. He came by with a sack of candy. I was outside in the front, and he told me to go in and get a bowl. Though I must have been around four, I still remember what the bowl looked like.

I remember Granddad's white hair, too. I used to sit on his lap and run my fingers through it. I remember sleeping on a quilt box at Aunt Iris's and hearing their mantel clock ticking and wishing I was home.

Uncle Bert was one of my favorite uncles. I loved the smell coming from his pipe. He always seemed to be using or cleaning his pipe. If I got close to him, he would catch me with the curve of his cane and pull me in toward him. I used to announce that I was going to smoke when I got big, even if I had to get behind the door to do it!

I always wanted to be a teacher; so I played "teacher" a lot. I remember wanting to have our cat as a pupil. I tried to put doll clothes on her, but she would always run away. I also made mud pies with Bantam hen eggs, just the really small ones that you can't do much with. I got them from Mother. Mixing them with dirt and water made wonderful pies, and I loved to play with them.

Mother was my teacher in first, second, and third grades because I went to a small country school where there was no other teacher. First grade was at Farmer School, while second and third were at Finney Switch. Once when I was in her class, Mother whipped me in front of everyone. I don't remember anything I had done wrong, and I think that she must have done it to teach the other students a lesson about what would happen if they did not mind. That incident made a huge impression on me.

When I moved to Plainview, I lived at a dairy. We had a dog named Collie. We always had dogs, but I remember Collie being a special pet. At the dairy we had dogs and chickens, and Daddy had cows.

We moved to 504 Oakland Street when I was starting the fourth grade, and that's when I met my best friends, Nelia Neis and Laqueta Chaney. Nelia lived directly in front of me, and Laqueta lived at the end of the block.

We had not met our neighbors until we started to church one Sunday. Daddy and Harold Neis both backed into the street at the same time and ran right into each other! Mr. Neis was so nice that I'm sure he and Daddy worked it out about that accident. That's how we all met.

We used to roller skate together and play together. I went on vacation with the Neis family because Nelia was an only child, and I helped fill in some gaps for her. Her father, Harold Neis, was a pharmacist.

504 Oakland Street was not a large house. We never lived in a very large house, because my parents couldn't afford it. My brothers slept in the back bedroom, and we did have one bedroom between their room and my parents' bedroom, where my sisters and I slept. The house had a living room and a small dining room and a small kitchen. It was painted white and not very attractive, but I'm sure it's what my parents could afford. There was very little land around it, only what you would consider a lot.

My parents always raised a garden. The one at the dairy was larger, but Mother and Daddy planted one at the Oakland Street house every year. Mother always canned the produce.

We also had an old ice-cream freezer, the kind where you had to sit on the lid. We used to fight over who would sit on the lid to hold the can down. We also fought over who would get to have the dasher out of the middle, as a lot of ice cream clung to the dasher.

Whenever we ate a meal, we all sat down together, all eight of us, and we said a blessing before the meal. Mother and Daddy would take turns saying the blessing. I really appreciated that it wasn't any kind of haphazard time. Mother expected us all to be together. It really bothers me how people eat now, sitting all over the house.

Daddy wasn't in really good health. He sold Watkins products at one time, vanilla and liniments and some other products of theirs. I don't remember him being really busy after we moved because of his health.

During middle school, I belonged to FHA, Future Homemakers of America. I was also in the choir at school for music class.

I belonged to a square dance club, and my friend Luther and I danced together. I had a fancy dress that matched his fancy shirt; so we always partnered together to dance for Old Settler's Reunions and gatherings like that because we had to match.

I loved school, and I never did want to do anything but teach school. After more than thirty years of teaching, I still do love to be around children. The only teacher I remember well is Mrs. Carter, my Home Economics teacher in high school. She was a big influence on my decision to become a Home Economics teacher.

For a teacher, I don't have very good handwriting, but Joyce and Grace do. Joyce always teases me about my bad handwriting, and I tease her right back that hers is only so good because she was a Journalism major.

One summer in high school, I sold shoes at Carl's Shoe Store on the weekends. Other than that, I did babysitting, lots of babysitting, just like Mother. Mother and Joyce and I all babysat often, and Mother sat for some families who used her for years. She did that at night and on weekends when she was not teaching.

I graduated from Plainview High in 1955. I am sure, looking back, that my leaving was hard on my parents, because I was the last child left. But I never knew anything about that at the time.

Leaving for college was not so bad for me. Nelia was my roommate; so it didn't feel like such a huge change. We both went to West Texas State College in Canyon all four years. It wasn't like leaving and not having people from home that I knew. I liked college and enjoyed my time there, and I don't remember ever being really homesick.

I liked my Home Economics classes and English literature. I grew up loving poetry because Mother read it to us all the time. The classes I didn't like were physics and chemistry, because I didn't feel like they pertained at all to my major. There were not enough Home Economics students taking science classes at one time to have a separate class; so Nelia and I (Nelia was a Home Economics major, too) had to take that class with the Physics and Chemistry majors. As I recall, neither one of us ever knew much about what the science teachers were talking about.

During college, I spent a summer working as a planimeter operator in Plainview. Each farmer was only allowed to have a specific amount of acreage planted in cotton, and if he had more, he'd have to plow it under. Of course, if he had more of an allotment than he realized, he could plant more. I looked at photos of the fields with a planimeter and figured out how much acreage each farmer had planted in cotton. That was a good job, and it was the best paying job I could find at that time.

While I was in college, I took a swimming class because I was determined to learn how to swim. I made a D, which is the lowest grade you can make and pass. Most of the other students were just taking it for a credit, and they already knew how to swim. I was just thrilled to pass. But I was still scared of the water.

In college, Nelia and I were in the Maid of Cotton contest; it was a beauty pageant that was a big deal in the area. Several schools participated, and Nelia and I were both nominees from our school. We didn't win, but it was a lot of fun. There were formal dresses and luncheons and things like that for the contestants, and it was all very interesting.

We both belonged to a Home Economics Club, where we met

and did various things together. Nelia and I both belonged to Chi Omega Sorority while in college as well. Because I was dating a Methodist, I would go to the Methodist prayer meetings after dinner each night. There would be singing and a small devotion.

I met Harold Lamb in the college cafeteria. There was just one place where everyone ate together back then. I started dating him when I was a sophomore or a junior. He was a year ahead of me in school and graduated a year ahead.

When we were dating, we'd spend some time at a nearby canyon where you could sit and talk and bring picnics. We went to movies sometimes, but there was only one theater, and the movies didn't change very often. We enjoyed playing tennis together.

Sometimes we went to Amarillo to have dinner. Though the college sponsored dances, we didn't go to them that I remember because I didn't know how to dance. The only dancing I had done was square dancing, not ballroom; I didn't know how to dance the other way.

Harold spent part of the year before I graduated in the Army. Harold gave me a really pretty ring, and I loved it. I graduated from college in 1959, and Harold and I were married in the fall.

The following spring, my mother died of cancer. She was only sixty-two. I did get to visit back and forth with her in the months before she died, but when she was gone, I missed her terribly.

JoAnn Virginia Schneider Lamb

CHAPTER ELEVEN (11)

The Four Winds

CHRISTMAS of 1952 was the last time the original Schneider family was together under one roof before any of the siblings married. It was the last time to feel that family closeness they had shared with the same people back on the family land in Farmer. By the next Christmas, Grace, Clyde, and Glen had all married, starting families of their own.

So we can understand how special this final time was for Laura. When she wrote of it, she titled it, "My Happiest Christmas." Here is what she wrote.

December 19, 1952

"JoAnn, jump right in bed while I get the hot water bottle and an aspirin." Then I will call Mr. Neis and ask him to bring a prescription from the drug store as he comes to supper. This was the first thing that happened when I got home from school the after-

149

noon of the 19th beginning the Christmas holidays.

We had had a very busy day at school. The gift exchange had worked out well, however. Each child had been given a generous treat by the room mothers and sent home with many good wishes for a happy holiday. When the books had been put away, the Christmas decorations taken down from around the room, flowers removed from danger of a possible freezing, and the thermostat set so for a comfortable heat in a closed room, I drew a deep sigh of happiness and closed the door on school room worries. Two whole weeks of happiness at home, just being "Mother," and the anticipation of having all my children at home together again.

After making JoAnn comfortable, I made a quick clean-up and pick-up over the house, went to the grocery store, and got supper under way.

Scarcely had I turned around it seemed before Daddy and Joyce came into the house laughing and I looked beyond them to see Martha giving Clyde's uniform a final check, with particular attention to the new wings just that day pinned on. Of course I said, "Greetings, Lt. Schneider," and in return got a big hug and saw the boyish grin of pleasure spread over his face. How a mother's heart swells with pride in such a splendid son!

After supper Daddy and I dashed off late to our Sunday School class social at the church. It was a delightful evening with old and new friends, and I went home with two gifts after Daddy gave me the box of ladies' hose he'd drawn in the gift exchange!

When we got home our first thought was of Grace, who was coming home with Carrie Bier. When they had not arrived by midnight we turned the fires low, left the door unlocked and a light burning, and went to bed.

Martha and Grace were to sleep in our room and Daddy and

I took the extra bed in the boys' room where Clyde was sleeping. About two o'clock Grace came in. She undressed very quietly, and not looking in Mother's room lest she disturb, went to the back bedroom to that seldom-used bed. She called softly, "Clyde, Clyde," and was startled to hear a movement in the bed that she was so sure would be empty.

Saturday morning brought the happy reunion of four children – Grace, Clyde, Joyce, and JoAnn, as well as Martha, the soon-to-be new daughter. A quick trip to town for last minute shopping, groceries, and a Christmas tree largely took up the morning. JoAnn and Clyde chose a beautiful, tall tree and began to decorate it even before the noon meal.

As the latter was almost ready, a quick wave of excitement ran through the house as someone called from the front, "Glendon has come." And there was the tall, sturdy jet pilot who had not been with us at Christmas time for the last three years. How glad he seemed to be at home again.

After having driven steady for the past 24 hours [from Alabama], he fell in bed as soon as he had eaten lunch.

Sunday was a happy day with church in the morning and callers [in the] afternoon. I sat with little Hal Seaman while his parents attended a rehearsal and dinner for a wedding party Sunday night but was back home in time for coffee with the family before bed time.

Again the light was left burning and the fires going because Finis would be coming in before morning. Daddy and I did not sleep very soundly and were awake when the car stopped in front of the house at 3:00, exactly 52 hours since they had left Red Bank, New Jersey. We knew he really wanted to be with us to make such a long, hard journey home. Christmas had already come in our hearts when the entire family gathered for a late breakfast on that beautiful Monday morning.

How quickly the days went until Christmas Eve morning when we wakened to find a beautiful blanket of snow covering the earth and what fun it was to go down town and see the gaily lighted windows, the throng of busy shoppers...

Here her writing ends. The last pages we can imagine: cooking the family dinner, opening presents, playing games, telling stories, and softly laughing with each other. We can picture the snow gleaming brilliantly outside the windows while inside, all is cozy warmth and friendliness and firelight.

Two days after that Christmas, Clyde married Martha. The couple left, and the rest of the siblings scattered to their homes. We've followed their lives to this point. We've seen Grace graduate and teach; Glen zoom upwards in the Air Force; Clyde learn to fly; Finis serve with honor and teach with enthusiasm; Joyce master pen and keyboard; and JoAnn dazzle everyone around her.

But what happened next? What did the grown Schneiders do?

-GRACE-

Grace taught third grade in Perryton, Texas from 1947-1948. Then she moved to Albuquerque, New Mexico, where she taught in 5 Points School from 1949-1952. She served her local church wherever she lived.

While in Albuquerque, Grace met a serviceman named Bill Winn, whom she married on June 20, 1953, in Plainview, Texas.

Bill received an honorable discharge from the Air Force, and the two of them moved to Maryland. There Grace taught third grade, while Bill worked for the Ralph M. Parsons Company.

In the autumn of 1954, Bill and Grace moved to Joplin, MO, for Bill's work. Grace taught school in Missouri, too. But the family's stay in Missouri was short.

Bill took a job in the summer of 1955 with Dow Chemical in Freeport, Texas. He and Grace moved to nearby Lake Jackson, Texas, which became their permanent home. Grace taught third grade in Brazoria, Texas.

Grace and Bill had two daughters, Kathy and Nancy, who were both born in Lake Jackson. Grace enjoyed raising them at home and being a mother instead of a teacher for a while. Grace and Bill both remained active at their church.

As Bill rose in the ranks of his work, he began to greet foreign executives and invite them into his home. There Grace befriended their wives, helping them to navigate American culture and learn English. So gracious and memorable was she at this work that many years later, when Glen met the same executives in Korea, the mention of Grace's name created instant goodwill.

Grace and Bill cared for Laura Schneider during her battle with thyroid cancer from 1959-1960. After Laura's death on April 12, 1960, Grace became a connector and center of care and affection for her siblings. She returned to her role as a kind of mother hen, only now, instead of teaching her brothers and sisters to read and helping to cook them meals, she cared for Joyce's sick child to give her sister a break, performed small kindnesses for other siblings as she could, and helped plan the family reunions that kept the Schneider siblings so close.

Toward the end of her father's life, Grace invited her father to live with her. He was not feeble; he cared for himself while he lived there and remained sharp-witted and able to the end. And during the nine years while he was living there, he wrote a few pages of memories, his and his father's, which Grace preserved and shared with her siblings. Carl Watson Schneider died at the age of ninety-six on July 30, 1985, after a stroke, and was buried near Laura in Plainview.

Grace's daughter Kathy married a doctor, and they moved for a while to Kenya as missionaries. Grace and Bill visited them there, spending three months. And Grace and Bill traveled other places as well, some in order to do church work and some just for the pleasure of traveling.

They went with the International Mission Board of the Southern Baptist Convention to Senegal to help with a construction project, to Russia for prayer walking, to Romania for church construction, to New Zealand to encourage the churches there, to Colombia for a conference and prayer walking, and to Belgium to work in a printing shop.

Besides their three months in Kenya, Grace and Bill spent thirteen months in the Philippines, eighteen months and then another seven months later in the Ivory Coast, and seven months in Mali. During these mercy trips, Grace has endured gunfire, earthquakes, volcanoes, and carjacking.

Grace and Bill traveled for pleasure to Japan, Korea, Israel, Egypt, Thailand, Singapore, China, Hong Kong, England, Greece, France, Switzerland, Norway, Denmark, Portugal, Germany, Sweden, Scotland, and Wales.

All the siblings have said that they were traveling to the places where their mother dreamed of going. Looking at Grace's trips across the globe, Laura would have been thrilled.

-CARL (GLEN)-

After Glen joined the Army Air Force in 1946, he began going by his first name, Carl. He served the Army Air Force through the last days of World War II, which officially ended by presidential proclamation on December 31, 1946, after the necessary military tribunals, prisoner repatriation, and demobilization of sixteen million men in uniform. Carl trained in Colorado, San Antonio, and Phoenix to fly aircraft.

During his early days in the service, a barracks corporal advised Carl not to volunteer for any extra work but just keep his head down and get by. But Carl rejected that advice in favor of the philosophy he'd developed on his father's farm and at his mother's knee.

Carl determined that he would do anything that made common sense, anything that was in the best interest of the service, and anything that no one could say benefited him personally. So Carl learned when he could bend regulations and take risks in the interest of efficiency or practicality. On the ground, Carl rose through the ranks rapidly.

In the air, however, Carl was a stickler for rules and regulations. In combat, he flew to the limit, but in peacetime he never believed that any training mission was worth taking unnecessary risks. He wanted to take no chances with his own safety or the safety of his aircraft or wingmen.

Bad weather or undue strain on his machine would send Carl to the nearest base to land. His caution won him the reputation of the number one overnighter in the service, but it kept him alive and saved valuable planes. In all of his flying, he never had an accident!

Caution did not equal a lack of courage, however. Carl flew over a hundred combat missions in Korea, fighting with daring and determination. He survived both the coldest Korean winter in a hundred years and the loss of twenty-two out of thirty-two pilots in his wing. Though the loss of many fellow pilots in that war was hard for Carl to bear, his early lessons in faith comforted him and kept him able to continue serving the Air Force.

Back in America, Carl moved from Phoenix to Las Vegas, Florida, and Del Rio. In Las Vegas, he met a beautiful young widow named Elaine and married her within three months, adopting her son Bob as his own. Carl and Elaine had another child, Debi, in 1956 at Offutt Air Force Base in Nebraska. Thanks to Elaine's steady, pleasant temperament and Carl's integrity, the couple remained happily married for more than forty-four years.

In the early fifties, Carl was assigned to exchange duty for a year with the US Marines at Quantico, near Washington D.C. While there, he had the opportunity to reunite with an old high school classmate, Jimmy Dean, who had become a famous country musician and television celebrity and who would eventually open a famous sausage factory back home in Plainview. At a dinner party, Jimmy Dean's wife played a demo record for Carl recorded by an up-and-coming-young singer Jimmy was trying to help: Elvis Presley.

Carl served in Germany, where he and Elaine and the children were able to travel to many places in Europe. He visited Africa, where he went scuba diving with a fellow pilot, Buzz Aldrin. Carl encouraged Buzz to go into space flight training.

Though Carl was selected for a program at Harvard, he received the news that his mother was ill with thyroid cancer; so he accepted an offer to continue his college education at the University of Texas, in an advanced management program. There, he was able to visit his mother often in Lake Jackson until she died.

After his time in Texas, Carl became an F-100 squadron commander in Arizona. From there, he was assigned to Vietnam and established the original Forward Air Controller/Air Liaison Officer system that was used throughout the rest of the war. He flew combat missions with the Vietnam Air Force and went on ground combat missions with the Vietnamese Army. Though he served faithfully, he was glad to return to America and his family.

Back home, Carl attended further college classes at Arizona State University. Finally, after nineteen years, he graduated with his college degree. He continued as a squadron commander at Luke AFB near Glendale until the Air Force transferred him to Fort Riley, KS, to the 1st Infantry Division as the Tactical Air Party Commander.

Carl next moved to Florida to fly F-4s, and there he had the pleasure of seeing his son join the Air Force. Carl next tackled the Air University and earned his master's degree. Then the Air Force sent him to Washington, D.C., where he became the executive officer to the assistant secretary of the Air Force for financial management, a bureaucratic position that tested Carl's patience.

Fortunately, Carl's next move took advantage of his active nature. He became the wing commander of an air base in Georgia. One of his students, training for the Texas Air National Guard, was a young man named George Walker Bush.

After Georgia, Carl and his family went to Korea, where Debi graduated from high school in Seoul. Then the family returned to Georgia, staying for only a while before they moved to Oklahoma City, OK, and then to Dayton, OH. In Dayton, Carl was the Chief of Staff Air Force Logistics Command (AFLC). He retired from the Air Force after thirty-two years of service as Major General Schneider.

He was awarded the Distinguished Service Medal, the Distinguished Flying Cross, and several air medals. After retirement, he was inducted into the Arizona Aviation Hall of Fame and the Arizona Veterans Hall of Fame.

After retiring from the Air Force, Carl turned his energy and the wisdom he had gained from his years on the Schneider farm and his years in the Air Force to business. He started, managed, and sold several businesses, enjoying success in the private sector in addition to his public service. He returned to his beloved Arizona, working in different business ventures and traveling often.

Elaine was an outstanding Air Force wife who never complained about the many, many moves Carl's job required. She ran their home efficiently and entertained their many friends and frequent distinguished visitors. Sadly, Elaine developed Alzheimer's. Carl cared for her devotedly for five years before her death in 1999. They had enjoyed a faithful, loving marriage for over forty-four years.

Carl remained in Arizona, returning to his business ventures and travel, and helping veterans where he could. He was on the founding board of the Joe Foss Institute, which educates children in civics and citizenship. He also worked with the Arizona branch of the Veterans History Project, which pairs veterans with high school students who carefully record the memories of veterans for posterity in the Library of Congress.

In 2001, Carl married again. Carole had worked in publicity in Manhattan and had ties to Arizona through her parents, and her calm and gentle nature reminded Carl of the best women he had known. The couple eloped to Hawaii, where they pledged faith in a private beachside ceremony. They have since celebrated fifteen years of travel and adventure.

Today Carl pursues various business ventures, travels to visit family, and helps veterans navigate the process of returning to the civilian sector, including working for veteran's programs at several colleges. He and Carole live in Tennessee, near Carole's daughter, and Carl travels to Arizona often for volunteer work and to attend meetings for several boards of directors.

-CLYDE-

Clyde graduated from Texas Tech in 1951 with a BBA degree, and very shortly afterwards, in June 1951, he reported to Lackland AFB for basic training. In October of the same year, Clyde trained at Hondo Air Base to fly T-6 aircraft, and at Reese AFB in Lubbock, he trained to fly B-25s. Then he flew transport missions in Korea at the end of the war.

Clyde married his wife, Martha Ann McNeill, on December 27, 1952, just a few days after the Christmas Laura described in "My Happiest Christmas." Like a lot of Air Force couples, Clyde and Martha moved multiple times across the country and the world following Clyde's training schedule and orders.

In Memphis, TN, Clyde learned to fly the C-119, and he and

the family moved to Ardmore AFB, OK so that he could fly them. Clyde and Martha's first child, Cindy, was born in Oklahoma on November 14, 1953. Next, flying C-119s took Clyde and his family to Greenville, SC.

In 1954, Clyde shipped overseas to Brady AFB, Japan, so that he could fly the C-46. Back in Lubbock, TX, Martha Carol was born on September 29, 1954 at Reese AFB. Then Clyde flew home to accompany Martha, Cindy, and Carol to fly to Japan. That November, the family moved to Ganosu, Japan, close to Ashiya AFB, where Clyde flew C-119s and C-47s.

Clyde and his family sailed home in November 1955, and he separated from the Air Force in December, though he stayed in the Air Force Reserve. He and his family settled in Lubbock, and on February 7, 1956, Susan Kay arrived to join the family.

Clyde invested with friends in Varsity Book Stores serving the Texas Tech students in Lubbock, where Clyde had attended college and graduated. The bookstores thrived and prospered, just as Clyde's family did. Clyde and Martha had another girl, Mary Lynn, on April 1, 1959. Also, Clyde became a charter member of the Southwest Lions Club in Lubbock, promoting charity and community improvement in the city.

On August 17, 1961, Martha and Clyde had a son, Allan Clyde. Martha was now the very busy mother of five children, a situation that seemed familiar to Clyde. Throughout the sixties and into the seventies, Clyde poured his energies into his family, his bookstores, and his charity work with the Lions. He rose to the position of Lions Club District Governor for District 2T2, covering the Lubbock area.

In the seventies, Clyde began flying again – recreationally this time. He soloed in a sailplane (glider) in 1970 at the Slaton,

Texas airport. In 1979, he even got a lesson in flying sailplanes from L.B. Schlemeyer, an old man who had taught Wiley Post to fly. (Wiley Post was the one-eyed aviator who was with Will Rogers when he was killed in Point Barrow, AK.) Schlemeyer had been the third pilot ever hired by TWA, and he had flown everything with wings. This distinguished pilot was at the same airport as Clyde to check out helicopters, but he granted Clyde the honor of a lesson when Clyde asked. He even signed Clyde's log book.

In 1973, Clyde left the bookstore business and moved with his family to Houston, TX to work for Grumbacher Company, an art supplies manufacturer and distributor. Having sold the company's products in his bookstores, Clyde already had a relationship with Grumbacher and knew the product. Clyde excelled at this second career, from which he retired in 1994.

Clyde has filled his retirement with family – a lot happens in a family of five children! He also flies sailplanes, and he and Martha have remained active in church. Clyde is a deacon in the Baptist church, and every year since 1993, he has traveled to Mexico to build churches, drill water wells, and install pumps.

He still likes to fix things. He and Martha bought an old farmhouse in the country, and Clyde spent years restoring it and improving it. The finished house was both authentic and lovely.

To be near their children and care for Martha's health, Clyde and Martha sold that house and moved to San Marcos, where they now live surrounded by loving family, in a house with a large workshop so that Clyde can keep fixing things.

-Finis (Frank)-

After high school graduation in 1948, Frank enrolled in West Texas State College, where he attended two years. Frank interrupted his college education to serve in the Army during the Korean War. He enlisted on January 22, 1951, completing his Army basic training at Fort Chaffee, Arkansas. He also completed Army Leadership School at Fort Chaffee.

He went from there to Fort Monmouth, New Jersey where he was in the first Signal Officer Candidate School class of the Korean War. Upon completion, Second Lieutenant Schneider was retained at the OCS as a Tac Officer. He supervised three succeeding classes of candidates through their programs of instruction. He completed his tour of duty there in 1953.

Then he re-enrolled in West Texas State College on September 30, 1953. While he was in college, he worked as a cameraman at a television station – KGNC-TV in Amarillo, Texas. The whole nation was opening to television at that time, and Frank excelled in the new, growing industry. Broadcasting, in both television and radio, tapped into his natural talent and honed skills.

Frank graduated from college in 1955 and returned to active duty in the Army in 1956. He reported to the Army Pictorial Center in New York City where he directed the making of training films for the Army. Following that assignment he completed the Photo Unit commander course, and Company Grade School at Ft. Monmouth, NJ. Later he also graduated from Command and General Staff College at Ft. Leavenworth, KS.

While climbing the ranks of the Army, Frank went to Iran to help the nation establish a television and motion picture industry. He built and ran Armed Forces Radio and TV station in

Iran. He directed one of the first national television programs on the Iranian television system.

Frank came home and returned to his military work. Happily, he met and married Eunice in 1962. She became a loving mother to Greg and Kim, and Frank and Eunice raised through their teenage years two more children from a previous marriage - Bradley and Laurie. From 1962-1964, Frank went to the University of Southern California, where the Army sent him to get his master's degree. His master's thesis was "A Historical Survey of the Development of Artificial Light Sources for Motion Picture Production."

Three years later, the Army ordered Frank to Vietnam, where he served as a Battalion Executive officer from 1967-1968. He earned a Bronze Star Medal for his duty in Vietnam, and over the life of his military career, he also won three Army Commendation Medals, a Joint Service Commendation Medal, and the Legion of Merit.

His military career took him up and down the east coast. In New York, he became a training film director. At the Pentagon in Washington, D.C., he was chosen as a staff officer twice. He was a TV director for QM school at Fort Lee, VA, and he was a staff officer in Fort Monroe, VA. Frank eventually retired from the Army in 1973 as Lieutenant Colonel Schneider.

Then he began a second career teaching broadcasting at Hampton University in Hampton, VA. He contributed to the community in Hampton, Virginia through teaching, broadcasting, and serving his church, Hampton Baptist Church, where he became a Life Deacon. Frank served as chairman of the board of deacons several times, was director of the Sunday school once, and taught Sunday school classes also.

He worked at Hampton University as a tenured professor until 1997. He interrupted his time in the classroom for two years, from 1975-1977, to earn his doctorate from the University of Texas. His doctoral dissertation was "An Examination of the Management Practices of Selected Independent, Non-Theatrical Motion Picture Producers in Texas." He also made training tapes as a visiting professor over two summers for NASA at Langley. In 1997, he retired from teaching, having won the distinguished teaching award at Hampton University, the distinguished service award from the Virginia Association of Broadcasters, and the Lily Fellowship from Colorado College in Colorado.

In retirement, Frank has enjoyed playing golf (until a back surgery interrupted), spending time with his family, and traveling. Over his life, Frank has traveled in Paris, Austria, the Czech Republic, Germany, Puerto Rico, Columbia, St. Martins, Quebec, Aruba, Canada, St. Thomas, Panama, Switzerland, England, Turkey, Iran, Belgium, Luxembourg, Guam, Saudi Arabia, and in all 50 states. If one child has been carried by the four winds to every corner of the world, Frank is that child.

-JOYCE-

After leaving home in 1950, Joyce worked for one year as a file clerk in Albuquerque. The next year, she attended UNM as a journalism major. But college life didn't suit her at the time; so she left UNM for work in the field she loved, writing for the *Albuquerque Journal*.

In 1954, she left Albuquerque to visit the family of a boyfriend in Pittsburgh, PA. After deciding against marriage to her Pennsylvania boyfriend, Joyce returned to Texas. It was thirty-two years before she returned to her favorite city of Albuquerque.

In Texas, she worked for a small West Texas weekly newspaper, the *Ralls Banner*. Then she moved to Amarillo and wrote continuity for KGNC radio station. At a church singles dance in Amarillo, she met Floyd Johnson, whom she married a year later, in 1957. He had entered college nearing the age of thirty, graduating with a degree in education.

The Johnsons moved to Houston, where Floyd taught school for a time. But he left teaching for work as a lumber salesman. While living in Houston, Joyce and Floyd adopted eight-year-old Eddy and baby Teresa. After the adoptions, the family moved near Beaumont, Texas, where they had a little boy, Andy.

In addition to raising her three children, Joyce edited the regional publication for Mayflower Movers in Dallas. The Johnson family moved to Rockwall, near Dallas, where they owned a lumber and builder's supply business. Joyce and Floyd enjoyed weekend property with cabins in both eastern Oklahoma and east Texas. They owned a motorhome and spent time in Colorado in addition to the weekend properties.

In 1982, the Johnson family was doing well personally and financially. But that year, Floyd was diagnosed with cancer. He died five months later.

Joyce stayed in Rockwall for four years after she lost Floyd. She kept busy working for the American Heart Association in Dallas until Andy and Teresa were both in college. Then she sold the house, her East Texas farm, and the lumber business, and she returned to Albuquerque in 1986.

Back in the city she had loved as a young woman, Joyce completed another year at the University of New Mexico. Four years after returning to New Mexico – at a square dance this time – Joyce met Bill Winn, an industrial electrician who invented go-carts, electric buggies, and devices for his electrical plant. They married in 1990 after a whirlwind courtship of only seven weeks and sent all their relatives into shock.

Joyce helped Bill realize his dreams of developing his inventions and learning to fly. He, in turn, enabled her to visit six other countries and to travel full-time in a motorhome after Bill retired. Joyce and Bill hosted national forest campgrounds in California and Colorado with other full-time RV travelers. Bill also enriched Joyce's life by making her stepmother to his four sons: Dennis, David, Dwayne, and Donald.

Fifteen and a half years later, tragedy struck Joyce's life once again. Joyce and Bill were hosting a campground in the mountains of California when Bill was diagnosed with cancer. Nine months later, in 2006, he died. For a time, Joyce remained in Albuquerque, where she could see the Sandia Mountains every day, because Albuquerque felt like home.

But in 2010, Joyce moved back to Texas. And who's to say where she will go next? According to Joyce, "I think I must be part gypsy. The other girls have each lived in their small towns for more than fifty years. I enjoy change and adjust to it easily. I can account for at least eight towns where I've spent periods of time. And that doesn't include three years of full-time RVing in three different states. I appreciate that we were raised in a stable, Christian home and were encouraged and supported in taking reasonable risks and trying new things."

Joyce is enjoying life in retirement. She loves travel, and since Bill's death, she has taken several trips with Elderhostel. She feels free to fly a kite, visit a zoo, play ping-pong, go bowling, read stacks of books, and do needlework. A Jack Russell terrier keeps her company when she is not visiting her family.

-JoAnn-

Harold and JoAnn worked together at the same high schools in Perryton and Aspermont. Harold was the football coach, and JoAnn was the Home Ec. teacher. They spent most of their time at the school. Because the schools were so small, Harold did a little bit of everything. In addition to coaching football, he taught basketball and baseball and track and field. The couple spent most of their time with school activities.

They always went to Sunday school and church. Because Harold was a Baptist, JoAnn became one, too. Laura had said that families should always go together for church membership.

The Lambs moved to Wellington, where JoAnn substituted in the school system. Lana Gail was born in Wellington in 1962. Then, in 1964, the Lambs moved to Andrews.

After they moved to Andrews, Harold started working for Amoco Oil Company. There wasn't an opening in the Andrews schools for a high school Home Ec. teacher; so JoAnn had to get re-certified to teach elementary school. She taught elementary school for a while, and then several years later, she opened a Home Ec. department in the middle school. JoAnn taught for eighteen years in Andrews.

When JoAnn had her daughter Lana, she kept working and had a sitter who cared for her. JoAnn loved being a mother, though she always felt like the family needed two incomes, and she loved teaching school as well. She had wonderful sitters over the years, mostly women from church, and she took the children over to their houses on her way to work.

JoAnn always wanted at least four children, but after Lana's birth she had some medical issues and couldn't have any more. Fortunately, the doctor she saw in Fort Worth told her that he'd help her and Harold get a child at the same home where he'd gotten his adopted child. Dr. Gordon, who was influential with the adoption agency, helped them to get a child a lot faster than they would have otherwise.

Harold and JoAnn adopted Jerry Dale in 1970 when he was only eight days old; so they were the only family he ever knew. Not too long ago, JoAnn and Jerry were talking about family, and she mentioned that he had the mother who bore him and then he had JoAnn. Jerry said, "Mom, you are the only mom I've ever had." JoAnn was so glad that her son felt secure and knew how much she loved him.

In 1978, when Jerry was eight and Lana was fifteen, Harold died of a massive heart attack. He was only forty-two – so very young. JoAnn's family was very helpful and very supportive and tried to see the Lambs as often as possible. No one can never replace a husband and father, but JoAnn's family tried to ease her loneliness as much as they could.

JoAnn's father was living with her at the time. He'd come to live with the Lambs before Harold died, and he stayed for a time afterwards until he went to Grace and Bill's house. Grace and Bill were very loving and kind to the whole family. Aunt Grace and Uncle Bill would get Jerry down on the floor and roll around with him and kiss him. He has very fond memories of Grace and Bill because of the way they just loved him.

The church was very important, too. Harold and JoAnn had close relationships in the church because they had always gone to church and taught Sunday school. At the time Harold died, he'd been teaching high school, and JoAnn had been teaching elementary school. Many good friends from church surrounded and loved her.

Of course, she had to lean on the Lord quite a bit, too, because of how hard it was to lose Harold.

After Harold died, JoAnn had the diamonds from her wedding ring reset into a dinner ring to wear. She kept teaching school, and she kept being a mother to her children. She stayed at the same church and reached out to her friends and the people who loved her.

In 1982, four years after Harold died, JoAnn married Bob Montgomery. He worked in the offices of Arco Oil Company, and he had two children, a boy and a girl. JoAnn had always wanted four children, and she hoped that she and Bob and their children would be a happy family together forever. Sadly, the marriage ended in divorce in 2006.

Though she retired from teaching full time in 1985, JoAnn continued to substitute in elementary school classrooms three or four days a week. Since she has had to deal with a broken leg and subsequent surgery in recent months, she has missed being in the classroom.

JoAnn loves to travel, and over her life she's been to eight foreign countries, including Belgium and Germany. Her favorite trip of all was to Alaska. She went with Grace and Bill, Glen and Carole, and with her childhood friend Nelia (who lives in California now). JoAnn loves spending time with her brothers and sisters and children and grandchildren.

JoAnn belongs to two bridge clubs, the DAR (Daughters of the American Revolution), and an association of retired teachers. She is also very active in her church. She has many friends and activities, though her activity has been limited lately because of her leg. Nelia, Laqueta, and JoAnn were best friends in school. They are still friends; both Nelia and Laqueta came to stay with JoAnn for a week after a surgery recently and helped her recover from a new hip and a broken leg. She is currently working hard at therapy (even in the water!) so that she can get well and strong again and do all the things she loves to do.

- LAURA'S BLESSING -

Laura was proud of all of her children. She looked at their lives, at the beautiful grandchildren and constant achievements, and she saw goodness. She saw lives worth giving hers to shape. And so Laura has the last word of all, in the words of her favorite poem by Canadian poet Anne Campbell.

TO MY CHILD[43]

You are the trip I did not take;
You are the pearls I could not buy;
You are my blue Italian lake;
You are my piece of foreign sky.

You are my Honolulu moon;
You are the book I did not write;
You are my heart's unuttered tune;
You are a candle in my night.

You are the flowers beneath the snow;
In my dark sky a bit of blue,

Answering Disappointment's blow
With, "I am happy! I have you."

ANNE CAMPBELL

Bibliography/Notes

THE Schneider siblings generously opened an entire archive of documents for this book, including photocopies of obituaries, genealogies, letters, recollections, photos, resumes, reunion games and lists, marriage licenses, insurance records, and essays written for college. Each sibling also answered interview questions emailed to them. All of these resources together formed a body of family history that supplements the individual papers and books noted in this archive. Though not all resources named here were quoted, all were helpful in providing background to the family story.

BOOKS

Dean, Joe. *Mother's Poetry: Poems by Flora Smith Dean*. Florissant, MO: publishing rights reserved, 1994.

Fairchild, Louis. *The Lonesome Plains: Death and Revival on an American Frontier*. College Station, TX: Texas A&M University Press, 2002.

Read, Hadley. *Morning Chores and Other Times Remembered*. Champaign, IL: University of Illinois Press, 1978.

Spikes, Nellie Witt, ed. Geoff Cunfer. *As a Farm Woman Thinks: Life and Land on the Texas High Plains, 1890-1960*. Lubbock, TX: Texas Tech University Press, 2010.

FAMILY ARCHIVES

Kerlin, John Peter, Obituary.

Ragle, Ernest. "Early Days in Lamb County." History 421 paper, West Texas State Teacher's College, January 15, 1937.

Schneider, Carl Watson, "History of Fred Ernest Schneider Family."

Schneider, Carl Watson, "Memories over Seventy-Five Years."

Schneider, Clyde Kerlin, CD recording, August 1989.

Schneider, Finis Earl. "A Pioneer of Crosby County." Paper, West Texas State College, March 1950.

Schneider, Finis Earl, ed., "Selected Letters Written to Laura Kerlin Schneider 1918-1926."

Thornton, SD, Obituary.

Winn, Grace Schneider, "For My Grandchildren."

INTERVIEWS

Lamb, JoAnn, phone interview recorded 7.6.16.

Schneider, Carl Glendon, personal interview recorded 4.8.16.

Schneider, Carl Glendon, personal interview recorded 3.25.16.

Schneider, Clyde Kerlin, tape recording received 5.4.2016.

Schneider, Finis Earl (Frank), personal interview recorded 9.12.16.

Winn, Grace Schneider, and Carl Glendon Schneider, Clyde Kerlin Schneider, phone interview recorded 4.27.16.

INTERNATIONAL RESOURCES

History.com. "The Dust Bowl." http://www.history.com/topics/dust-bowl (accessed 7.10.16.).

Pohly, John. *Active Rain.* "Real Estate History: Robinsonville to Robinson, The Prestigious Waco (TX) Suburb." October 22, 2007, http://activerain.com/blogsview/245824/real-estate-history--robinsonville-to-robinson--the-prestigious-waco--tx--suburb- (accessed 7.10.16.).

Perryton, TX: Wheatheart of the Nation. "Black Sunday." http://www.perryton.com/black.htm (accessed 7.10.16.).

Texas PBS. "Texans and the Dust Bowl." http://texaspbs.org/dust-bowl/ (accessed 7.10.16.).

Texas State Historical Association (TSHA). "Dust Bowl." https://tshaonline.org/handbook/online/articles/ydd01 (accessed 7.10.16.).

The USGenWeb Project. "Crosby County: Joseph Jefferson Spikes and Nellie Witt Spikes." http://www.rootsweb.ancestry.com/~txcrosby/ralls/s/spikes_nellie_jj.html (accessed 7.10.16.).

US Air Force. Biographies: Major General Carl G. Schneider. http://www.af.mil/AboutUs/Biographies/Display/tabid/225/Article/105674/major-general-carl-g-schneider.aspx (accessed 7.10.16.).

Wikipedia, s.v. "Alderson, West Virginia," https://en.wikipedia.org/wiki/Alderson,_West_Virginia (accessed 7.10.16.).

Wikipedia, s.v. "Dr. Pepper," https://en.wikipedia.org/wiki/Dr_Pepper (accessed 7.10.16.).

Wikipedia, s.v. "Dust Bowl," https://en.wikipedia.org/wiki/

Dust_Bowl (accessed 7.10.16.).

Wikipedia, s.v. "Görlitz," https://en.wikipedia.org/wiki/ G%C3%B6rlitz (accessed 7.10.16.).

Wikipedia, s.v. "Giddings, Texas," https://en.wikipedia.org/ wiki/Giddings,_Texas (accessed 7.10.16.).

Wikipedia, s.v. "Lee County, Texas," https://en.wikipedia.org/ wiki/Lee_County,_Texas (accessed 7.10.16.).

Wikipedia, s.v. "Ralls, Texas," https://en.wikipedia.org/wiki/ Ralls,_Texas (accessed 7.10.16.)

Wikipedia, s.v. "Waco, Texas," https://en.wikipedia.org/wiki/ Waco,_Texas (accessed 7.10.16.).

Wikipedia, s.v. "Wends," https://en.wikipedia.org/wiki/ Wends (accessed 7.10.16.).

ENDNOTES

---

[1] Louis Fairchild, *The Lonesome Plains: Death and Revival on an American Frontier* (College Station, TX: Texas A&M University Press, 2002), xvi.

[2] Nellie Witt Spikes, Geoff Cunfer, ed., *As a Farm Woman Thinks: Life and Land on the Texas High Plains*, 1890-1960 (Lubbock, TX: Texas Tech University Press, 2010), 17.

[3] Ernest Ragle, "Early Days in Lamb County," (History 421 paper, West Texas State Teacher's College, January 15, 1937), 6-7.

[4] Finis Schneider, "A Pioneer of Crosby County," (Paper, West Texas State College, March 1950), 2-3.

[5] Spikes ed. Cunfer, *Farm Woman*, 18-19.

[6] Joe Dean, *Mother's Poetry: Poems by Flora Smith Dean* (Florissant, MO: Publishing rights reserved, 1994), 21.

[7] *Wikipedia*, s.v. "Görlitz," https://en.wikipedia.org/wiki/ G%C3%B6rlitz (accessed 7.10.16.).

[8] Carl Watson Schneider, "History of Fred Ernest Schneider Family," (Lake Jackson, TX: unpublished memoir, n.d.), 1.

[9] Clyde Kerlin Schneider, personal memoir CD recording, Houston, TX: unpublished, August 1989.

[10] *Wikipedia*, s.v. "Giddings, Texas," https://en.wikipedia. org/wiki/Giddings,_Texas (accessed 7.10.16.).

[11] *Wikipedia*, s.v. "Lee County, Texas," https://en.wikipedia.org/wiki/Lee_County,_Texas (accessed 7.10.16.).

[12] *Wikipedia*, s.v. "Wends," https://en.wikipedia.org/wiki/ Wends (accessed 7.10.16.).

[13] *Wikipedia*, s.v. "Waco, Texas," https://en.wikipedia.org/ wiki/Waco,_Texas (accessed 7.10.16.).

[14] *Wikipedia*, s.v. "Dr. Pepper," https://en.wikipedia.org/ wiki/Dr_Pepper (accessed 7.10.16.).

[15] *Wikipedia*, s.v. "Alderson, West Virginia," https://en.wikipedia.org/wiki/Alderson,_West_Virginia (accessed 7.10.16.).

[16] C.W. Schneider, "History," 1.

[17] John Pohly, *Active Rain*, "Real Estate History: Robinsonville to Robinson, The Prestigious Waco (TX) Suburb," October 22, 2007, http://activerain.com/blogsview/245824/real-estate-history--robinsonville-to-robinson--the-prestigious-waco--tx--suburb- (accessed 7.10.16.).

[18] C.W. Schneider, "History," 1.

[19] Obituary of SD Thornton.

[20] Obituary of John Peter Kerlin.

[21] All of the following stories are from the CK Schneider CD.

[22] Fairchild, *Lonesome Plains*, 4.

[23] Schneider, Finis Earl, ed., "Selected Letters Written to

Laura Kerlin Schneider 1918-1926," (Hampton, VA: unpublished, 1998) letter from Una Kerlin to Laura Kerlin and Mae Kerlin, Tuesday, September 30, 1919, letter 7.

[24] Obituary of John Peter Kerlin.

[25] F. Schneider, "Letters," letter from Una Kerlin to Laura Kerlin, Wednesday, September 17, 1919, letter 37.

[26] Carl Watson Schneider, "Memories over Seventy-Five years," (Lake Jackson, TX: unpublished memoir, n.d.), 1.

[27] Proverbs 27:10 KJV

[28] C.W. Schneider, "Memories," 2.

[29] C.W. Schneider, "History," 1.

[30] C.W. Schneider, "History," 2.

[31] Fairchild, *Lonesome Plains,* 16-17.

[32] C.W. Schneider, "Memories," 3.

[33] C.W. Schneider, "History," 2.

[34] C.W. Schneider, "Memories," 3.

[35] Isak Dinesen, http://www.brainyquote.com/quotes/authors/i/isak_dinesen.html (accessed 7.10.16.).

[36] C.W. Schneider, "Memories," 2.

[37] Clyde Schneider, tape recording received 5.4.2016.

[38] Grace Schneider Winn, "For My Grandchildren."

[39] Schneider genealogy.

[40] C.W. Schneider, "Memories," 2.

[41] Clyde Schneider, 1989 CD.

[42] Joe Dean, *Mother's Poetry,* 48.

[43] Anne Campbell, "To My Child," trustyoureditor.com/post/12605885483/from-to-my-child-by-anne-campbell (accessed 7.10.2016).

[44] Virginia Moore, "Family Ties," http://www.dennydavis.net/poemfiles/fmly1.htm. (accessed 9.22.16).

Photo Gallery

Family Ties[44]

Family ties are precious things,
Woven through the years,
Of memories of togetherness,
Of laughter, love and tears.
Family ties are cherished things,
Forged in childhood days,
By love of parents, deep and true,
And sweet familiar ways.
Family ties are treasured things,
And far though we may roam,
The tender bonds with those we love,
Still pull our hearts toward home.

Virginia Moore

JACKSON,   WACO, TEX.

Our paternal grandparents, Frederick Ernst & Elizabeth Virginia Bare Schneider, as a young, married couple.

Our paternal grandparents, Frederick Ernst & Elizabeth Virginia Bare Schneider, and their family. Our father, Carl Watson Schneider, is second from the left on the back row.

Our maternal grandparents, John Peter Kerlin & Launa (Una) Thornton Kerlin, and their family. Our mother, Laura Kerlin Schneider, is the far right on the back row.

*Our paternal grandfather,
Frederick Ernst Schneider.*

*Our maternal grandfather,
John Peter Kerlin*

*Frederick Ernst Schneider's
grave & most of mother's...*

John Peter Kerlin

Our father, Carl Watson Schneider,
as a young soldier in World War I.

Emma Schneider English (left) &
Laura Kerlin Schneider

Our parents, Carl Watson &
Laura Kerlin Schneider,
on their wedding day.

Carl Watson Schneider (back row), Laura Kerlin Schneider
(front right), and Aunt Docia (front left)

Left to right: Carl Watson Schneider, Clyde, Grace, Laura Kerlin Schneider, Joyce (in Mother's arms), and Glen (Carl)

Left to right (front row): Laura Kerlin Schneider, Carl Glendon Schneider, Clyde Kerlin Schneider, Finis (Frank) Earl Schneider, John Robert Nance Back row: Iris Kerlin Vernon, John Peter Kerlin, and May Kerlin Nance

*Carl Watson & Laura Kerlin Schneider at train depot
in Omaha, Nebraska at Christmastime*

Carl Watson & Laura Kerlin Schneider with a grandchild

*Carl Watson & Laura Kerlin Schneider's house
as the Schneider children remember it. Left to right: Carl
(Glen), Clyde, and Frank (Finis).*

Laura Kerlin Schneider (1950)

SCHOOL DAYS 1956-'57
Seth Ward Elem.

*Laura Kerlin Schneider,
the teacher.*

Carl Watson Schneider with his sisters

Anna Schneider Ragle, Carl Watson Schneider, Emma Schneider English, Ellen Schneider, Minnie Schneider, Albert Ragle, Orville English, Fred Schneider

Back Row: JoAnn, Joyce, Finis, Clyde, Front Row: George Ragle, Priscilla Ragle, Laura Schneider, Carl Watson Schneider

Carl Glendon Schneider sitting on the running board of his parent's car

Carl Watson Schneider watering the garden

Carl Watson Schneider

Carl Watson & Laura Kerlin Schneider
with Carl Glendon Schneider in 1952

Our father, Carl Watson Schneider, (center)
with his children: Frank (Finis Earl), Alma Grace,
Launa Joyce, JoAnn Virginia,
Carl Glendon, and Clyde Kerlin in the back

*Carl Glendon & Elaine Schneider; Martha &
Clyde Schneider; Laura & Carl Watson Schneider*

Our father, Carl Watson Schneider

Carl (Glen) Schneider as a baby

Carl (Glen) on his 3rd birthday

Carl on Jellybean

*Left to right: Carl (Glen), Clyde,
and Finis Schneider*

*Left to right: Grace, Carl (Glen), Clyde,
Finis, and Joyce Schneider*

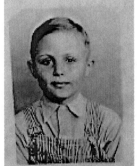

Finis (Frank) Schneider

Joyce Schneider &
Finis (Frank) Schneider

JoAnn Schneider Lamb
at 2 years old

Grace & Glen Schneider

Ruth English with cousins

Cousins at Uncle Orville's

JoAnn Schneider, Joyce Schneider
& Clydene Mitchell

Launa Joyce

Cousin Jonell English

Alma Grace Schneider Winn
(high school photo)

Carl Glendon Schneider
(high school photo)

Clyde Kerlin Schneider
(high school photo)

Frank (Finis Earl) Schneider
(high school photo)

Launa Joyce Schneider Johnson-Winn

JoAnn Virginia Schneider

Carl Glendon Schneider
in Korea (1950)

Frank (Finis Earl) Schneider standing at
attention on right receiving an award

Clyde Kerlin Schneider with Uncle Fred
and Aunt Ellen

Clyde Kerlin Schneider & Cousin Jo

(Left to Right) Carl Watson & Laura Kerlin
Schneiders children: Carl, Clyde, Frank, JoAnn,
Grace, and Joyce

Carl Glendon & Elaine Schneider

Elaine Schneider

Carl Glendon & Elaine Schneider with
Debi Schneider

Left to Right: Joyce, JoAnn & Grace

Front Row: Joyce, JoAnn, Grace
Back Row: Finis, Glen & Clyde

Bill & Grace as newlyweds

Eunice Schneider & son Greg

Frank (Finis Earl) & Eunice Schneider, Kim & Greg

Floyd Johnson (1956)

Bill Winn (1998)

Launa Joyce Schneider Johnson-Winn

JoAnn Schneider

Harold Lamb (husband of JoAnn Schneider Lamb)

*Front Row: Martha Schneider (holding baby Cindy Schneider),
Laura, JoAnn, Grace, Joyce - Back Row: Clyde, Glen,
Carl Watson, Finis & Bill Winn*

Clyde & Martha Schneider

Carole & Carl Glendon Schneider

Major General Carl G. Schneider USAF

Carl Watson Schneider

The Schneider children today (left to right): JoAnn,
Frank (Finis), Grace, Joyce, Clyde, and Carl (Glen)

A Few of Carl G. Schneider's
Favorite Veteran Organizations

...

JOE FOSS
INSTITUTE

A Few of Carl G. Schneider's
Favorite Books

...

Life Application Bible
Wounded Tiger (Martin Bennett)
The Fourth Fisherman (Joe Kissak)
A Proud American (Joe Foss)
Duty (Robert Gates)
A Higher Call (Adam Makos)
Gods Word For Warriors (Tom Seals)
The Art of Leadership (Robert E. Lee)
Sergeant to CEO (Sean P. Jensen)
Lincoln On Leadership (Donald Phillips)
Flying High (Stowe Dailey-Shockey & Calvin Lehew)
Things That Matter (Charles Krauthammer)
Cassada (James Salter)
No Dream Is Too High (Buzz Aldrin)
Duty Honor Country (George Day)
Delta Blues (Dr. Terry Smith)

GOD'S
WORD FOR
WARRIORS
Returning Home Following Deployment

THOMAS L. SEALS

@ amazon.com

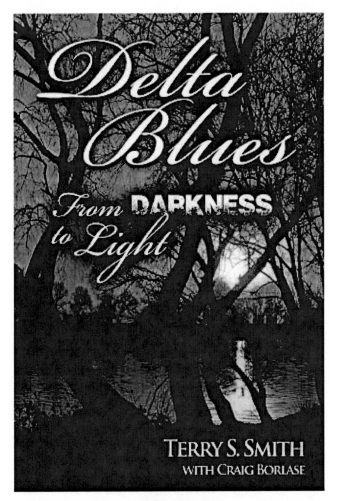

TERRY S. SMITH

WITH CRAIG BORLASE

coachinglifematters.com

VIETNAM SAGA

Exploits of a Combat Helicopter Pilot

Stan Corvin, Jr.

vietnamsaga.com

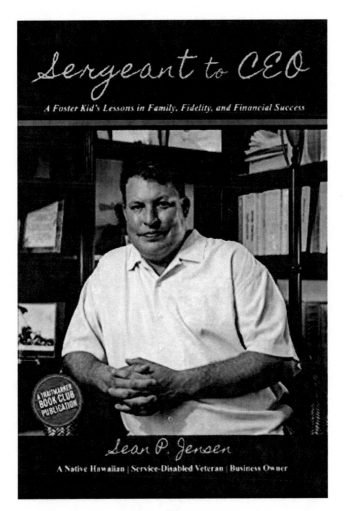

Sergeant to CEO

A Foster Kid's Lessons in Family, Fidelity, and Financial Success

A TRAITMARKER BOOK CLUB PUBLICATION

Sean P. Jensen

A Native Hawaiian | Service-Disabled Veteran | Business Owner

sergeanttoceo.com

FOREWORDS BY NAOMI JUDD
& RITA DAVENPORT

flying
high

a true story of
shared
inspiration

*If you are ready to fly high in health,
happiness, wealth and a deep joy of living,
read my friend Calvin's book...*
MARK VICTOR HANSEN
bestselling author, *Chicken Soup for the Soul*

CALVIN LEHEW
STOWE DAILEY SHOCKEY

flyinghighbook.com

Coming in 2017 ...

Jet Pioneer: A Fighter Pilot's Memoir

Jet Pioneer: A Fighter Pilot's Memoir is the chronicle of the military life of Major General Carl Schneider from his enlistment as a private, his rising through the ranks, and his journey from aviation cadet to his service as a jet fighter pilot in the Korean War. It also includes his various operational and command assignments including his service in Vietnam where he set up the USAF Forward Air Controller program in the early 1960s. It concludes with his senior military promotions and his role Chief of Staff of the USAF Logistical Command.

Carl G. Schneider with Stan Corvin

Carl Schneider's first jet fighter (F-84) at Shaw AFB, SC (1948)

CPSIA information can be obtained
at www.ICGtesting.com
Printed in the USA
LVOW07s0609020517
532923LV00001B/404/P